What Difference Does it Make?

April 17,
2002

Dearest Megan —

Your Grandfather Dave worked with
this book's author's father, Paul Little.
We're sure you will find it
useful along the way as you
seek to live for Jesus.

Love and Happy Birthday!

Grandfather Dave and
Gms

What Difference Does It Make?

Adapted by Debi Brazzale
Illustrated by David Sullivan

Equipping Kids for Life!
faithkids.com

Faith Building Guide can be found on page 160.

Faith Kids® is an imprint of Cook Communications Ministries,
Colorado Springs, Colorado 80918
Cook Communications, Paris, Ontario
Kingsway Communications, Eastbourne, England

WHAT DIFFERENCE DOES IT MAKE?

First printing, 2002
Printed in the United States
1 2 3 4 5 6 7 8 9 10 Printing/Year 06 05 04 03 02

Editors: Jeannie St. John Taylor and Heather Gemmen
Designer: Keith Sherrer, iDesignEtc.

contents

CHapteR one

What book has been read by more people and translated into more languages than any other book?

HiNT

Try to imagine who could write the most important book ever. Each and every word of this awesome book is inspired by someone who is powerful beyond our imagination. It's his autobiography. The book he wrote provides us with the information we need to find out who he is and what he is about. In it he tells us what he is like—he reveals himself to us.

But he did not write the words down himself: he had a variety of people to write down his thoughts. These writers were so impressed with the book they were writing that they said many wonderful things about it. They said it was

- honey in my mouth
- a lamp for my feet
- a joy and delight to my heart
- a fire that burns in my heart
- more precious than gold

THE BIBLE

What book has been read by more people and translated into more languages than any other book?

If you guessed the Bible, then you would be right.

Believe it OR NOt

Most people *in* the Bible never *read* the Bible.

They couldn't, since much of the Bible hadn't been written yet. They experienced God in other, different ways. God made sure that they knew everything about him that they needed to know. He sent prophets to speak his words, and he commanded parents to tell their kids about him so they could tell their kids and they could tell their kids.

However, since God finished writing the *Old* Testament more than four hundred years before Jesus came to earth, many copies of it were available in New Testament times. Jesus, along with many other young boys, not only read it, but also memorized huge sections of it. Jesus called it "scripture."

The people who wrote the Bible didn't *know* they were writing it.

Over a period covering more than 1,600 years, God put words into the minds of more than forty writers. They wrote down what God wanted them to say, not knowing that their words would later be part of the Bible. The apostle Paul wrote letters to his friends; the prophet Jeremiah gave God's warnings to a king. The personalities and experiences of the writers all show in their writings.

Because God inspired each and every word, we can be sure that there are no mistakes in the Bible. And through the years, God protected each and every copy that came from the original writings. At first the copies were all carefully copied by hand, later people pecked out the words on typewriter keys, and now Bible publishers use computers.

The Bible contains some evil words.

Some parts of the Bible contain the words of evil and foolish people—even of Satan himself. These parts are simply true pictures of the people's words and circumstances. For example, in the Old Testament there is a book called Job. It is the story of a man who lost everything he owned and loved after Satan and God argued. The book quotes God's words, the words of Satan, the words of Job, and the words of Job's friends. God wanted us to know Job's story, so he inspired the writer to record it accurately, even though terrible things happened and were said.

The Bible says God keeps the world from exploding.

God is the one who keeps the world going. Scientists have learned that light travels in waves and that there are certain characteristics of light. These light waves travel at incredibly high speeds. But who or what keeps it in motion? What makes light travel? Scientists don't have an answer to these questions. Scientists can only figure out how things work, but they can't explain why things work. The Bible says that God is in command of the universe. God causes light to travel. Science without a Christian viewpoint is limited in what it can teach us. The Bible teaches us why the universe is as awesome as it is. If God were to remove himself from our world it would no longer function: light would stop traveling, gravity would no longer keep our feet on the ground, and the earth would fall apart. You might want to stop and thank God that he keeps things going for us every day.

- More than forty men wrote the sixty-six books that make up the Bible.
- The earliest was written about 1,110 years before Jesus' birth; the last book, Revelation, was written about 100 years after Jesus' death.
- The people who wrote the Old Testament wrote in Hebrew, the language of God's chosen people: the Jews.
- Jewish people wrote the New Testament as well. But they wrote in Greek, the language most people used in New Testament times.
- The Jews translated the Old Testament into Greek and arranged the books in an order that made sense to them. Our Bible today is in that same order.
- Though these writers lived more than a millennium apart, they all said the same things about who God is and who Jesus is.
- Jesus, who claimed to be God, often quoted the Old Testament. Almost one-third of the New Testament is made up of quotes from the Old Testament.
- The Bible contains the actual words Jesus said while he walked around on our planet.
- About 400 years after Jesus, many Christians lived in Rome and spoke Latin. So they translated the Bible into Latin.
- In 1214 A.D., Christians divided the Bible into books, chapters, and verses with numbers.
- Finally, it was translated into most of the languages of the world and now is available at your local mall, bookstore, or webstore.

- Archeologists are people who learn about ancient civilizations by digging up buildings, tools, and pottery that were buried long ago. Archeologists first started digging sometime in the early 1800s.
- They found pharaohs of Egypt lying in solid gold coffins, they found names and places from the Old Testament written on palace walls, and they found Babylon—the place where Daniel spent some time with lions and lived to tell the tale. Their discoveries proved that many of the events and people talked about in the Bible were true accounts.
- More than 25,000 sites (that's archeological sites, not web sites!) have been connected to the Bible—and many more sites are still unexplored.
- Archeologists dug up three cities that date back 4,100 years, to the time of Abraham: Mari, Nuzi, and Alalakh. They found a royal palace that had more than 260 rooms. They found writing tablets that told us what their daily lives were like and how families lived. All these things helped prove what the Bible says about Abraham and his family.
- Solomon, according to 1 Kings, was a very wealthy king in Israel. Archeologists found some sites that prove Solomon had access to a lot of gold.
- In 2 Kings, a story of a war between Israel's King Joram and King Mesha of Moab is told. Archeologists found a stone that related the whole story—just like in the Bible. You can go and see the stone if you can talk your parents into taking you to the Louvre museum in Paris, France.

- Daniel, the dreamer and the lion tamer, said he knew a king named Belshazzar. Other records claimed Belshazzar was not the king, but that it was another guy named Nabonidus. Well, archeologists found more ancient records proving Daniel was right after all. He was so right that an archeologist stated that chapter five of Daniel's book in the Bible is the most accurate account of this part of history.
- The earliest part of the New Testament was written in 40 A.D., ten years after Jesus died. The reason that this is important to know is because it shows that the events that took place around Jesus were fresh in the writer's mind. And remember, they didn't have video cameras to preserve their memories back then. Writing was important, especially accurate accounts of what really happened. The Bible that we have now is taken from these writings.
- Most of the discoveries that prove the truth of the New Testament are writings on papyrus or broken pieces of pottery. Some discoveries are as ordinary as shopping lists—but exciting because they prove that the Greek language was spoken then. Papyrus copies of all four Gospels have been found. One copy of the book of John dates back to the year 100 A.D.
- The books in the Bible that we have today were written 100 years after Jesus was born—and archeologists have found 5,500 copies from that time.
- So far, nothing written in the Bible has ever been proven wrong by archeology.
- Archeological findings have proved that specific biblical events people used to laugh at—saying, "That couldn't have happened!"—are completely true.
- Learning about the world in which the Bible people lived has given us a better understanding of why

things happened the way they did. With the new information, archeologists solved several mysteries from the Bible. And who doesn't love a good mystery solved!

Ask Professor Little

Q: What makes you so sure the Bible isn't full of mistakes?

A: That is an excellent question. Don't kiss your brains good-bye just because you've been told to believe what's in the Bible. Scribes copied the earliest manuscripts onto parchment skins that were rolled into scrolls. They were obsessed with doing it perfectly. They actually counted the letters on each copy to make sure that all copies had the same number of letters. If they found a mistake they would throw the whole thing out and start over. They knew that they were dealing with the Word of God, so they even wiped their pen clean each time before they wrote the name of God.

Q: How do we know the right books were included in the Bible?

A: We accept the Bible as it has been handed down throughout history. The scriptures in the Old Testament were considered to be the Word of God when they were written, and they were passed on as such. Christians in the early church agreed on which writings they considered New Testament scripture. In one of his letters, Peter calls the apostle Paul's writings "scripture." The Bible as we know it comes from about 367 A.D. when the church made it official. Nothing has been added to the Bible since shortly after Jesus went up to live in heaven. Ultimately, God is the one who will show you whether it is his Word or not.

Q: Can you believe in the Bible and science at the same time?

A: God is the creator of our planet and the universe. He knows a bit about science. Not only did he create everything, he designed everything and he knows where he placed every cell, molecule, atom, and every fraction of an atom. He knows all the answers to every science question ever asked. Scientists, on the other hand, are often baffled. Science is a fascinating look into the world that God made. Some scientists are Christians and some are not Christians. Sometimes scientists disagree, especially about how the world came into existence. The Bible doesn't give the kind of answer that you might find in a science book but it does tell us who made the world and why he made the world. I guess God just figured that since he gave us brains he would let us have the fun of learning how the world works. The first people to use the scientific method—which is asking a question, guessing an answer, testing the answer, and making a conclusion—were Christians. God made the universe so perfectly and orderly that it was worth investigating, so they launched a whole new way of learning about God's world. They believed in the Bible and enjoyed science.

Q: What do you think is the most exciting archeological discovery so far?

A: That's easy. It's the Dead Sea Scrolls in 1947. This discovery wasn't even made by archeologists, though; it was made by a goat herdsman who was wandering around some caves in the sides of the cliffs near the Dead Sea. I don't know where his goats were but he did find some rolled-up leather scrolls in the caves. It turns out that these are the original Hebrew scriptures. These were the original originals. In these scrolls they found every book of the Bible except one. They were almost word for word the same as the Hebrew scriptures that we have now from those perfectionist scribes. Amazing, huh?

Q: So does archeology make the Bible true?

A: We do not believe the Bible because of archeology. That would be foolish. But archeology does provide evidence that supports what the Bible says. It also cannot prove the existence of God (as if they could dig up God!). God doesn't need archeologists to prove that he exists. No, he'll just show up when you go looking for him.

Q: Is everything in the Bible true?

A: The Bible contains language that is both literal (just the facts, like a geography book) and figurative (creating a picture, like J. R. R. Tolkien's *The Hobbit*). When Jesus says "I am the door," he doesn't mean he's actually a door; he means that knowing Jesus is the way we get in to see God. When Isaiah said, "The trees of the fields will clap their hands," he was just trying to make a point about joyfulness. Sometimes the colorful language writers use is meant to create an image in your mind—to help you see what they see. Also, it's very important to read more than just a few words so that you know what they're talking about. For example someone once read a line from Psalms that said, "There is no God." The problem was that he forgot to read the first part of the sentence that said, "The fool says in his heart—there is no God." Oops!

BeSiDeS THaT...

- When we read the Bible, we get to hear what Jesus was like from people who actually hung out with him while he was here on earth.
- The Bible has motivated people to create beautiful art, to sing and dance, and to write literature. The Chronicles of Narnia by C. S. Lewis was inspired by the Bible.
- A remarkable number of prophecies in the Bible have been fulfilled. The Bible says if a prophecy turns out to be false, it was spoken by a false prophet.
- The Bible says that:
    1. God existed before the universe.
    2. Time has a beginning.
    3. God created the universe from things we can't understand.
    4. God designed the universe so we could live here.

What Difference Does It Make?

The difference between reading the Bible and not reading the Bible is:

Growing more or not growing more into a relationship with the God who made us, who loves us, and who most definitely wants us to know him.

Remember:

- The Bible is kind of like God's instruction book for living.
- God tells how the world was created and how we came into being.

- God wrote a whole book to tell us how much he loves us and what he has planned for us.
- People who read the Bible and want to hear God's voice speaking to them will hear that voice.

(Scripture passages to support this chapter)

Believe It or Not

- Jesus refers to OT as scripture—Mark 12:10–11
- God inspired scripture—2 Timothy 3:16

Besides That. . .

- False prophecy = false prophet—Deuteronomy 18:22

CHapteR

two

Is there a God?

HiNT

Even though "God" is one of the most commonly used words in our language, many people wonder if he even exists. Throughout human history, from the people of Noah's time, to you and your friends, people keep asking that question because they *want to know the answer.* It's important.

But many people get their ideas about God all mixed up. They think of him as a superhuman force, a ball of fire ready to consume us, a mushy old grandpa in the sky, or a celestial policeman waiting for us to mess up. Albert Einstein said that God is "a pure mathematical mind." These are all interesting ideas, but none of them are true.

God is who he is no matter who we say he is. If you really want to know who he is—and whether or not he exists—you must study the evidence. It is an important question that has a yes-or-no answer.

GOD

Is there a God?

Yes. And he wants to reveal himself to you...

Believe it oR NOt

God reveals himself through nature.

Have you ever swum in the ocean, walked through a forest, or hiked in the mountains? Do you have a special pet like a dog or cat or a gecko? No human could ever create anything as awesome as nature. The tallest building in the world cannot compete with a mountain. God created these things and through them tells us that he is good and wants us to enjoy his creation. Steve Irwin the Crocodile Hunter is expressing his awe of creation when he is wrestling a crocodile and declares, "She's a beauty!" The natural world is a wonderful thing—filled with interesting places to explore and strange creatures to enjoy. And they all teach us a little bit about God.

God reveals himself through history.

History can be another word for story. The story of the Jewish people cannot be told without mentioning God. In fact, most of the Old Testament is the story of the Jews. God was involved in their individual lives and in the life of their nation. He talked to them, he took care of them, he punished them to bring them back to him when they disobeyed, and he even helped them fight wars.

This is the same God, thousands of years later, who involves himself in *our* lives.

God reveals himself through words.

The prophets of the Old Testament were always going around saying things like, "This is what the Lord said," or, "The word of the Lord came to me." They heard what God said and told everyone who would listen. Thousands of years later, God's words spoken through the prophets still call out to us from the pages of the Old Testament.

Have you ever conducted an experiment using the scientific process? First you ask a question, then you state what you think is true, then you prove it true or false by experimentation. Many people only believe a thing to be true when they can prove it scientifically. Can we prove God exists by scientific method? No. God cannot be put into a test tube or displayed at a science fair. But is it necessary to prove that God exists by the scientific method? No. Did Mozart exist? Yes. Can it be proven by scientific method? No. We know that Mozart lived because of his works and the words other people wrote about him. Those things witness that he existed. Just because we can't see someone doesn't mean she doesn't exist.

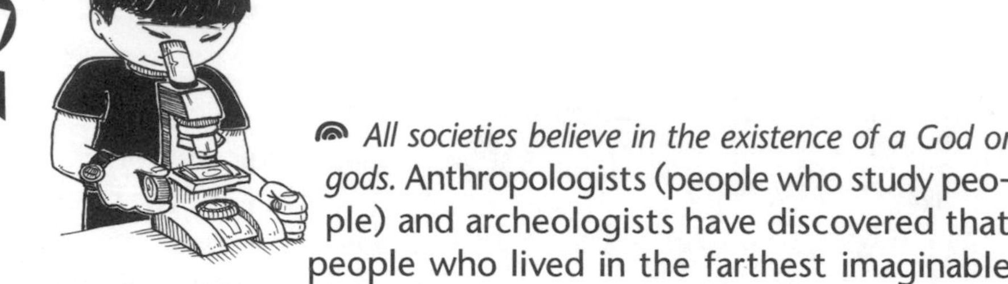

- *All societies believe in the existence of a God or gods.* Anthropologists (people who study people) and archeologists have discovered that people who lived in the farthest imaginable places and in the most ancient times share a common belief in some kind of a god. God placed a longing for him into our hearts.
- *We're here.* We had to come into existence or we wouldn't be here. Right? Where did we come from? We have parents, of course, and they had parents, and they had parents.... But where did it all start? Someone must have created the first person. It started when God created Adam.
- *It took a brilliant being to create the whole world and make it work perfectly.* Even Einstein recognized the "presence of a superior reasoning power." Einstein was pretty smart himself, but only God is smart enough to create the world (or an Einstein!).
- *The world couldn't have sprung into being by accident.* Imagine shaking up a bag of Legos® and dumping them out. Would each piece fall into just the right place, connecting together perfectly to create a beautiful Lego® creation? No way! Just like the Lego® example, way too much thought and detail went into the design of the universe to say that it all began just by chance.
- *Every detail of creation has a purpose.* Gravity keeps us from flying off the face of the big round ball we call earth. Newton discovered gravity, but he didn't invent it—God did. Every molecule, every atom, every weird-looking microscopic critter has a purpose, a function, and cannot be or do anything that it was not meant to be or do. Only God could program a world that requires so much cooperation from each of its parts.
- *Many scientists think that a theory called the Big Bang explains how the earth began.* That theory says the world came into being sud-

denly, in a single (and probably loud!) moment. It also tends to prove the truth of the biblical account in Genesis. God merely spoke aloud and the earth popped into existence. A very big BANG is likely.

- *People have a built-in sense of right and wrong.* Have you ever had someone butt in front of you in a line? Or has anyone broken a promise to you for no good reason? You immediately knew those things were wrong, didn't you? Every human being on earth knows the difference between right and wrong. Some societies may have different rules and standards, but the same basic idea of right and wrong (morality) exists in every society. God put that knowledge of right and wrong in our hearts.

- *God talks to people.* God spoke in the Bible; he speaks today. Sometimes people hear him in their thoughts and sometimes he speaks through messengers such as prophets, angels, or preachers. He speaks in dreams, on mountaintops, in deserts, in the wildernesses, during the night, and during the day. It's hard to deny that someone exists when he talks to you.

- *God changes people.* Even a real jerk can become nice when he meets God. Bullies stop bullying; liars stop lying; robbers stop robbing. Somehow they change. If you ask one of these people why she has changed she has only one explanation. God changed her.

ZOOM OUT

- Scientists everywhere agree that our universe had a beginning. Scientists do not agree, though, on *how* it began.
- The theory of evolution is an attempt by scientists to explain how the universe and our planet earth got where they are today. But the problem with evolution is that it doesn't have a beginning that can be explained—unless a god existed to put into motion the evolutionary process.
- Some people believe that God created the universe over time and that science allows us to have a peek into the marvel of the creation process. Other people believe that God simply spoke the universe into existence creating an instant world. Poof!
- People throughout the ages have kept track of time. First they used fancy hourglasses and sundials, then clocks, and finally watches that beep. But watches don't keep time unless someone sets them. Sundials had to be placed where the sun shines. These timekeepers merely keep track of time and tell us when to have lunch—they are not time itself. Time keeps going and going like the Energizer Bunny whether we keep track or not. Think about this—does time have a beginning? A zero hour? Who set time into motion in the first place?
- God doesn't need to wear a watch or look at clocks because everything happens in one eternal moment for him. He can see everything that has happened and everything that will hap-

pen all at once. He doesn't even have to take the time to rewind or fast forward. Pretty cool, huh?

* Genesis says God created the world in six days and on the seventh day he rested. But we really don't know how long that took because we don't know the length of God's days. The Bible says that to God one day is like a thousand years and a thousand years like one day. Wow! This could give a whole new meaning to "Have a nice day"!

Q: What's the coolest thing about God?

A: I can think of at least three things about God that are very cool. First, *God is omnipotent,* which means he is all-powerful. The Bible says that the universe itself speaks of the power of God. Picture the Rocky Mountains or the huge crashing waves of the oceans. God made them and rules over them. Imagine yourself cruising through outer space in a spaceship. God made the heavens and rules over it as well. Nothing is impossible with God. He can do anything he wants to do—although he decided on certain things he could never do (like lie). God is more than supersized. God rules and is supreme!

Second, *God is omnipresent,* which means he is everywhere at once. No matter where you go, he will go with you—to the peak of Mount Everest, the middle of the Pacific Ocean, the North Pole, the South Pole, and everywhere else in between. He is also at your house, at your school, and at your friend's house. No place on the face of this earth or in outer space is too distant for God.

And third, *God is omniscient*, which means he knows everything. He knows every kind word and every mean word you speak. He knows your every thought and action. It is impossible to hide anything from God. He knows what you are thinking about before you think it. He not only knows this about you, but also about every person on the face of this earth. That's a lot of stuff to keep track of!

Q: Does God just hang out in heaven?

A: No. God occupies our world. God did not simply set the universe in motion like a windup toy and then kick back as if he were at the movies enjoying popcorn and soda. He is very interested in his creation and wants to be involved.

Q: Since he has decided to come down and join us does this mean that he is not supreme anymore?

A: No. Fortunately God can be both supreme and with us at the same time. The reason he can is because he *wants* to be with us and he can make that choice because he's—well—supreme. But it is important to remember that God is still greater than his creation and he is the source of our life. We are not his equal but he still wants to be with us.

Q: Where does God come from?

A: *God is eternal and timeless.* He never had a beginning and will never have an end. Could anyone or anything have created God? No. No one or nothing could have created God. God always existed. Because of this, *God is limitless, not controlled by anything.* God can do anything he chooses. No one tells God what to do. Also, *God is unchangeable.* He is who he is. He isn't fickle and always reinventing himself. Sometimes he changes his mind, but never his nature.

Q: Does God have a body?

A: *God is spirit.* He doesn't have a body like ours, but he is real and he has a personality that we can observe. But did you know that the Bible says that we are made in *his* image? In fact, next time you find yourself staring at someone, look for the image of God in him.

Q: What is God like?

A: *God is holy.* He is totally perfect and everything he does is good. Evil deflects right off him. He cannot tolerate even the tiniest speck of sin anywhere near him because he's so incredibly holy. *God is loving.* His love is a perfect love. If anyone were to ask you to define the word *love* you should send her directly to the nearest Bible. God's love is all over It. God's love is full of action. His creation was an act of love. Sending Jesus to be born and to die was an act of love. Jesus' whole life here on earth was about loving people.

BRaiN StRaiN

1 + 1 + 1 does not always equal 3.

- God the Father + God the Son (Jesus) + God the Holy Spirit = 1 Person
- God is one being but exists in three persons. This is called the Trinity.
- Although we say "persons" it is important to know that the Trinity is not three individuals, but three elements that work together for the same purpose.
- This is not just a theory a human being concocted to explain why God is the way he is; this is what God says about himself.
- Think of it as God the creator expressing his love for us through Jesus with the Holy Spirit as the activator. In the Old Testament, the Hebrew word for God was in the plural form.
- In the New Testament, Jesus taught his disciples to baptize in the name of the Father and of the Son and of the Holy Spirit.

It's a good thing that God is three persons because it makes him easier to get to know. We can see God in the world he created. We can relate to God through his Son Jesus, and we can connect to God through the Holy Spirit. All you have to remember is that sometimes 1+1+1 equals 1. (Just don't use this kind of addition on your next math test.)

BRaiN StRaiN

Think of counting as high as you can. . .then add another number, and then another, and another. . . . Now count backwards, past zero into the negative numbers, as far as you can; and then subtract one more, and then another, and another. . . . There will always be another number. This is eternity.

As the Apollo 8 spacecraft circled the moon for the first time in 1968, astronaut William Anders read from Genesis, "In the beginning God created the heavens and the earth. . . ." Even astronauts know the work of God when they see it.

What Difference Does it Make?

The difference between believing in the God of the Bible and not believing is:

Discovering or being unaware of all he has to offer us.

Remember:

- Even if we don't believe in him, God still exists.
- God loves us whether or not we love him.
- God knows us better than we know ourselves.
- God wants us to know him.

(Scripture passages to support this chapter)

Zoom In

- God put the knowledge of right and wrong in our hearts—Romans 1:18–20

Check It Out

- Nothing is impossible with God—Mark 10:27
- God is omniscient. He knows every thought and action—John 2:25
- God is omnipresent. He is everywhere—Psalm 139:1–16

Brain Strain

- Jesus told his disciples what to say when baptizing—Matthew 28:19

CHaPteR

three

Was Jesus really the Son of God?

HiNT

Jesus claimed he was the Son of God, but many people down through the ages didn't believe him. They agreed that Jesus was a great teacher, a good and moral man—but not *God.* Other people believed that Jesus was exactly who he claimed to be—the Messiah, the Son of God. But they admitted it was a hard thing to prove.

Suppose someone were to write a story today about a famous person who recently died, like Princess Diana. If they claimed she was God, forgave people's sins, and rose from the dead, no one would believe it—because too many people are around that knew Princess Diana. The biblical accounts of Jesus were originally written and read by people who were around when Jesus lived. Those people knew the truth about him.

Jesus Christ

Was Jesus really the Son of God?

Absolutely. Jesus told the truth about who he was, and backed it up with action—awesome action.

Believe it oR NOt

How to love an ant.

Suppose you wanted to tell a colony of ants how much you loved them. (Sounds reasonable, doesn't it?) How would you go about trying to communicate with them? The best thing to do would be to become an ant. Then you could enter their colony and tell them in ant language how much you love them. That is what God did for us. He visited our planet and became one of us so he could show us how much he loves us.

A baby born in a barn rocks the world.

God made himself visible by sending his only Son down to earth as a baby so we could see him, touch him, and know he existed. This was no ordinary baby. This was the Son of God. The same God who created the universe. The same God who decided that you would be you. The same God whose creation chose to step into a big, disgusting pile of sin.

God gave this baby a mother named Mary who became pregnant through the Holy Spirit. She gave birth to him in a stable, in the small country town called Bethlehem. Mary and her husband Joseph gave the baby the name God chose for him: Jesus.

Jesus had a stepfather named Joseph (who was Mary's husband) and several younger brothers and sisters. Jesus grew up in this family—a kid just like you. He worked as a carpenter, just like his dad, Joseph. But this was no ordinary kid. This was part of the Trinity, God on earth. This was God's Son whom he sent to earth to love us. His coming rocked the world. His birth split time in two.

Jesus: all God, all human, all the time.

If Jesus was just a man and not fully God, the whole foundation of Christianity would have crumbled and withered away within a short period after Jesus left the earth. We'd still be living under Old Testament rules because no one would have had any reason to write a New Testament about Jesus. But Jesus was God living inside a man's skin. God became a man.

The Jewish religious leaders hated Jesus because he claimed to be God. They refused to believe he was who he said he was. They hated him when he claimed he had God's authority. He said that he could forgive sins, he said that he had the authority to judge us, and he said that he could raise the dead. The religious leaders knew only God could do those things.

Only Jesus could do God's job.

When some guys heard that Jesus was teaching in someone's house, they thought they would bring a friend who was paralyzed and ask Jesus to heal the man. But the place was so packed—people crammed into every space in the house, sitting on each other's laps and peering through windows and doors—that they couldn't get even a foot in edgewise. Since they weren't about to turn around and head home, they climbed up onto the roof, cut a hole in it, and lowered their friend to Jesus.

If the people weren't shocked when this guy came down through the roof, they were certainly shocked at what Jesus said to him, "Your sins are forgiven." This sent everyone up in arms because only God could forgive sins. Then, to *prove* he was God, Jesus healed the man—who promptly stood up and walked away.

- Jesus was present when God created the earth. As a matter of fact, Jesus helped create the earth.
- Jesus was already God's Son before the creation of the earth.
- Jesus tried to tell some folks that he knew Abraham. They thought that was the most ridiculous thing they had ever heard. They said Jesus would have to be four thousand years old if that were true.
- Since Jesus is God, he is *omnipotent* (all powerful), *omniscient* (sees everything), and *omnipresent* (everywhere at the same time).
- Have you ever felt really hungry or thirsty? Jesus went without food for forty days and became *very* hungry.
- Do you ever get tired? Jesus often walked "a day's journey," about twenty miles, and needed to rest at the end of the day.
- Have you ever been angry? One time Jesus got so mad at people who were selling things where they shouldn't be that he knocked over tables and chased them out.
- Have you ever cried? Jesus looked out over the city of Jerusalem and cried because he knew its people would suffer.
- Have you ever dreaded doing something? Jesus sweat drops of blood the night before he hung on the cross.
- Do you feel bad when someone else is having a bad day? Jesus had compassion on the people who swarmed around him.
- Are there people that you love and would miss if they were gone? Jesus cried when his friend Lazarus died.

ZOOM OUT

✦ If you want to find out about a well-known person, you might read about him in a magazine, watch an interview on TV, or go to his web site. If you want to know about someone in your class or on your soccer team, you talk to her and ask her questions. But the best way to find out who she is is to just come out and ask her. So . . . who did Jesus say he was? The Son of God. Plain and simple.

✦ Jesus knew everything that would happen to him before it happened. He knew all about the more than three hundred prophecies from the Old Testament that spoke of him. He even read some of them to people.

✦ The Old Testament contains many prophecies about Jesus. They tell us how his life would go. Prophesies said that:

He would be born in Bethlehem
He would help people
He would be sold for 30 pieces of silver so the police could arrest him
He would remain silent when he was arrested
He would be condemned with criminals
He would be crucified (hung to die on a wooden cross)
His side would be pierced
He would have a raging thirst when he died
He would be buried by a rich man
He would be dead only three days
He would become alive again

✦ Jesus was born in Bethlehem, helped others, was sold, was arrested, didn't say a word, was condemned as a criminal, was crucified, was stabbed with a sword, asked for water, died, was buried in a rich man's tomb for three days, and rose from the dead. See any similarities?

- The Jesus we worship and believe in is alive—not mummified and on display in a museum.
- Because Jesus rose from the dead we won't have to stay dead either. When he comes back to get us, our bodies will be resurrected as well. (More on this in chapter 10. It's pretty cool!)
- God knew that Jesus' death was necessary to atone (pay) for our sins and reconcile us to God. The death of Jesus made it possible for God to restore us to what he had originally intended for us. So he allowed it to happen. He knew it would happen. He planned it that way.

1. A man in England in the 1930s decided to write a book proving Jesus did not rise from the dead. But after researching and looking into the evidence, he had to change the title of his book—*because the facts convinced him that Jesus did rise from the dead.*

2. The Bible records that Jesus called himself the "Son of Man" (meaning, human) eighty times.

Q: Did Jesus lose any of his power when he became a man?

A: Jesus had all the power. One time Jesus was in a boat and a huge storm came; Jesus stood up and commanded the wind and the waves to stop blowing and crashing—and they obeyed! Imagine the weather report *that* night on the evening news! Another time Jesus came across a blind man and he made him see again. He had power, all right.

Q: Was Jesus really perfect?

A: Yes. Jesus Christ was perfect. He never sinned, not even once. He even challenged people to prove that he had sinned.

Q: Why was it so important for Jesus to be perfect—sinless?

A: Only a perfect person could pay for our sins. Jesus stood up for us and become an acceptable sacrifice for our sins.

Q: Why couldn't God just forgive us? Did Jesus have to die on the cross?

A: Sin cannot be soaked up with forgiveness. All wrongdoing requires punishment. But God's love is amazing: he loves us so much that he couldn't stand to punish us. He let Jesus take the punishment instead.

<Factoid>

When soldiers arrested Jesus, the disciples, who had been Jesus' best friends for three years, suddenly turned into frightened cowards, just like the lion in *The Wizard of Oz.* They all deserted him. Peter was so afraid he even lied and said he didn't know Jesus. But then, after Jesus rose from the dead, all his disciples became roaring lions as they ran around announcing, "He is risen!"

Pop Quiz

Jesus claimed he was the Son of God. This tells us that Jesus was one of four things.

Which one is right?

A. **Jesus was a liar**
B. **Jesus was a wacko**
C. **Jesus was a legend**
D. **Jesus was telling the truth**

Was Jesus a liar? Not likely. Even people who say that he is not the Son of God believe that Jesus was a great moral teacher. These same people agree that telling a lie is not a moral thing to do. So if Jesus lied when he called himself the Son of God, Jesus could not have been a moral person.

Was Jesus a wacko? Everything that was written about him suggests that he was a normal human being and that all his ducks were in a row. Even when he was under a lot of stress, he didn't lose it.

Was Jesus a legend? Legends are stories that evolve and change as they are told and retold over many years. Archeologists have proven that the accounts of Jesus written by Matthew, Mark, Luke, and John were all written about the same time—during the lifetime of people who actually knew Jesus. These accounts were more like newspaper stories than legends; and they have not changed over time.

Was Jesus telling the truth? If he wasn't a liar, a wacko, or a legend, then he was telling the truth, the whole truth, and nothing but the truth. And he would have sworn it on a whole stack of Bibles if they had been printed yet.

Investigate: "And, Please, Just the Facts, Ma'am"

Theory: The people who saw Jesus resurrected were hallucinating because they wanted so much for him to be alive. They only imagined that they saw him.

Fact: If so, that would mean hundreds of people in several different places at several different times were having identical hallucinations. That is not possible.

Theory: Jesus' followers lied about seeing him alive.

Fact: Many of them were killed for claiming that Jesus rose from the dead. Nobody is stupid enough to die for a lie.

Theory: Jesus' followers stole the body.

Fact: Armed Roman guards were stationed outside the tomb.

Theory: The authorities moved the body.

Fact: The authorities didn't *want* the body moved. Their worst nightmare was that the tomb would be empty.

Theory: The disciples looked in the wrong tomb. Jesus' body was still in a different grave.

Fact: If that had happened, the authorities would have pointed out their mistake and produced the body from the right tomb.

Theory: Jesus wasn't dead at all, but fainted and was buried alive. He later just walked away.

Fact: He would have needed to squirm out of seventy-five pounds of cloth wrapped tightly around him like a mummy, move the massive boulder blocking the entrance to his grave, fight off several guards, and walk away after nearly bleeding to death three days earlier.

Theory: Jesus is dead.

Fact: Jesus is still alive today.

BeSiDeS THaT...

- Jesus stayed on earth for forty days after the resurrection in order to prove to his followers that he was really alive. He appeared to them every now and then. Once he talked to two people walking down the road, another time he popped up in the midst of five hundred people. One of the last things he did on earth was cook breakfast: While the disciples fished from a boat, Jesus appeared on the beach and made a fire. When they came ashore for breakfast, he fed them cooked fish.
- Jesus came as a baby born in a stable, worked as a carpenter, and spent one of his last days on earth hanging out on a beach, cooking fish, with his closest friends: grubby fishermen. That was Jesus, the Son of God, hanging out with his creation.
- After Jesus died, came alive again, and spent some more time with his disciples, he was taken to heaven—and so he completed the job he came to do: to save us from death. With Jesus sitting beside God's throne, we're allowed to boldly enter the throne room; all we have to do is pray. And because of Jesus, God sees us as holy and blameless.
- The Bible says Jesus is still in heaven, preparing a place for us to live with him.

When Jesus died, he died as a man. God did not die. When we die our bodies die, but our soul and spirit continue to live. Jesus experienced human death, but then even his physical body came alive again.

Name Game

Jesus — the name given to him at birth

Christ — "the anointed One" in Greek

Messiah — "the anointed One" in Hebrew

So what does anointed One mean?

It means this is the only person for the job.

King of the Jews — a political title given by other rulers

Lord — master or ruler

Savior — a person who saves others

Son of God/Son of Man — he was God's son born from Mary's human body

Lamb of God — God's sacrifice

Teacher — one who helps us learn

Rabbi — a Jewish religious leader

Shepherd — he takes care of us

<Factoid>

Jesus was no ordinary person. He was the Son of God—but he hung out with all the wrong people (sinners, lepers, workers, ordinary people). He spoke out against the corrupt religious leaders and their practices, and he performed miracles. Author Don Everts puts it this way in his book, *Jesus with Dirty Feet*:

Jesus was loved
Jesus was hated.
People either
Gladly dropped
Everything
To follow him,
Or they spat in disgust
And plotted his murder.
His words were too clear,
His life too stunning,
His actions too miraculous
For those who saw him and his dirty feet
To respond in any other way.

What Difference Does It Make?

The difference between believing that Jesus is the Son of God and believing that Jesus was just a man is:

Getting to know someone who is alive or learning facts about someone who is dead.

Try to remember back to a time you did something really bad. You knew your parents would punish you. Think about how you felt. Remember the dread and the distress as you waited for it to happen. Now imagine someone walking in and announcing that he would take your punishment instead of you. You are free to go play and he will stay behind and be punished. It would seem too good to be true. That is what Jesus did for us by dying on the cross.

(Scripture passages to support this chapter)

Believe It or Not

- Jesus is fully God. He said, "I and the Father [God] are one."—John 10:30
- Jesus forgave sins—Luke 5:20

Zoom In

- Jesus was present when God created the earth—Colossians 1:16
- Jesus never sinned—Hebrews 4:15

Zoom Out

- Jesus would be born in Bethlehem—Micah 5:2; Matthew 2:1
- Jesus would be sold for 30 pieces of silver—Zechariah 11:12; Matthew 26:15
- Jesus would remain silent when arrested—Isaiah 53:7; Matthew 27:12–19
- Jesus would be condemned with criminals—Isaiah 53:12; Matthew 27:38
- Jesus would be pierced—Zechariah 12:10; John 19:34
- Jesus would have raging thirst when he died—Psalm 69:21; John 19:28
- Jesus would be buried by a rich man—Matthew 27:57–60
- Jesus would stay dead only three days—Jonah 1:17; Matthew 12:40
- Jesus would become alive again—Psalm 16:10; Acts 2:31

REWIND

Chapter 1

- More than 40 writers wrote the Bible over a span of 1,600 years.
- We can trust the Bible because God inspired every word, then scribes carefully kept the copies free from error.
- Archeological findings have proven the truth of many specific biblical events.

Chapter 2

- God is *omnipotent* (all-powerful). Nothing is impossible for him.
- God is *omniscient*. He knows everything.
- God is *omnipresent* (everywhere). He will be with you wherever you go.
- God, Jesus, and the Holy Spirit are one being who exists as three separate persons. This is called the Trinity.

Chapter 3

- Jesus was present when God created the earth; God created the earth through Jesus.
- Jesus was both fully God and fully human.
- Jesus died on the cross for our sins, rose from the dead, and is still alive today.

CHaPteR four

What do breath, wind, fire, oil, and water have in common?

HiNT

They are all used to describe a being in the Bible. He has a personality, he can think, and he has feelings. He can make choices. He is eternal (will live forever) and he is omnipresent (everywhere). God wouldn't be God without him. Jesus said that blasphemy (an insult) against this being is worse than blasphemy against himself—and is the only sin that God will not forgive.

the HOLY SPIRIT

What do breath, wind, fire, oil, and water have in common?

They are all words that describe the Holy Spirit.

The Holy Spirit is our comforter.

Jesus said the Holy Spirit is our comforter (not the kind you put on your bed!). He is like a best friend who is always there when we are feeling sad and alone. He comforts us when no one else can.

The Holy Spirit is our counselor.

When we need advice, the Holy Spirit teaches us things and reminds us of things that Jesus said, just in case we forgot.

The Holy Spirit helps us understand himself.

He helps us understand what we read in the Bible, and he points out things we need to know. We start by looking at what the Bible says about who he is and what he does, and then let him do the rest. It is a good idea to ask him to help you understand the Bible every time you start to read it. We need the Holy Spirit to help us understand himself, because that's part of what he does—he helps us understand things.

The Holy Spirit is equal to God and Jesus.

This is called the Trinity. The Trinity is: God the Father + God the Son (Jesus) + God the Spirit (the Holy Spirit) = One Person. If this is difficult to understand, maybe it would help to think how something ordinary, like water, can exist in three forms. Water can be ice (solid), water (liquid), or steam (gas). Each form has its individual characteristics, yet each form is water.

The Holy Spirit talks to people.

Once the Holy Spirit told this guy Philip to go walk beside the chariot of a man from Ethiopia who wanted to know about God. Philip obeyed, and the man ended up believing in Jesus and getting baptized. It's in the Bible, in the book of Acts (chapter 8), if you want to check it out.

What does the Holy Spirit do?

Reveals Jesus
Comforts us
Counsels us
Gives us wisdom
Prays for us
Gives us power
Helps our weaknesses
Gives spiritual gifts
Gives spiritual fruit
Convicts us
Lives in us

The Holy Spirit talks to God for us when we don't know what to say.

Have you ever wanted to tell somebody something and you just couldn't think of the right words? Wouldn't it be great if someone who knew just the right thing to say could speak for you? Well that's what the Holy Spirit does. The Bible says that he takes our prayers to God with groanings we can't even understand.

Names of the Holy Spirit:

Spirit of Truth
Spirit of Wisdom and Understanding
Spirit of Counsel
Spirit of Power
Spirit of Knowledge
Spirit of Promise
Spirit of Glory

The Holy Spirit is the one who convicts us of sin.

The reason that we feel bad when we've done something wrong is because the Holy Spirit is at work in us.

The Holy Spirit convicts us of what is righteousness.

Righteousness is having nothing to hide from God. The Spirit makes sure that we know how to become righteous.

The Holy Spirit convicts us of judgment to come.

When the Holy Spirit convicts us of our sin and how unrighteous we are, it should send us running to Jesus—which is an excellent thing because that is exactly where we need to be. If we are standing alone when judgment comes we are in big trouble because we need Jesus to make us righteous and to get rid of our sin for us.

- The Holy Spirit gives us gifts. These aren't your average under-the-tree Christmas gifts or fad-of-the-week birthday gifts. These are spiritual gifts that he gives to all Christians.
- In a letter he wrote to members of a church in Corinth, the apostle Paul lists the gifts the Holy Spirit gives. He said the Holy Spirit gives the gift of:

  wisdom
  knowledge
  faith
  healing
  miraculous powers
  prophecy
  discernment
  speaking in different tongues
  interpreting tongues

- The Holy Spirit gives these gifts as he wishes.
- Some of them may sound mysterious and you may wonder why they are even called gifts. But all these gifts are necessary for the church to be healthy.
- The Spirit makes sure that everyone gets the right gifts so he can share his gifts with the whole church.

- The Holy Spirit has been around a long time—for eternity to be exact. But in our earth-time he was alive and well, doing his work, even way back in those wild and woolly Old Testament days.
- The Holy Spirit helped with the creation of the universe. Genesis says that he "hovered" over the waters.
- The Holy Spirit gave wisdom and skill for particular jobs to particular people in the Old Testament. Warriors were given power and judges were given wisdom. One stunning moment, the Holy Spirit helped Samson rip a lion's jaws apart! Another time, the Holy Spirit filled a craftsman named Bezaleel (if you can't pronounce it, just call him Bez) so he could create beautiful works of gold, silver, and bronze to decorate the tabernacle (a beautiful tent where the Jews worshiped God).
- The Holy Spirit inspired the prophets. Sometimes they would start their messages from God with "The Spirit came into me," or "I heard him speaking to me." In the New Testament, Paul says that the Spirit spoke through the prophets.

- Once, when King David told God sorry for doing something really bad, he begged God not to take the Holy Spirit away from him. He wanted to do right, and he knew that he needed the Holy Spirit's help to do it.
- Much of the Old Testament looks forward to the day when Jesus would come. Along with this promise of Jesus were promises of a Holy Spirit outburst. Through the prophets, God said things like: "I will pour out my Spirit on your children and on their children," "I will pour out my Spirit on all people" (not just the Jews), and "I will pour out my Spirit in those days."

Throughout the Old Testament, promises about the Holy Spirit as well as promises of Jesus' coming were made over and over. Kind of like a two-for-one deal.

Q: Why did David have to beg the Holy Spirit to stay with him? Isn't he always with us?

A: In the Old Testament, when the Spirit came to individuals it was on a temporary basis. He came, did his job, and then left. It was not the same kind of relationship you have with your friends. He would just show up, hang around for a while, and then go away. After Jesus left the earth and went to heaven, he sent the Holy Spirit to his people just as he said he would—and the Spirit has been with us ever since.

Q: Didn't the people in the Old Testament miss having him around?

A: Yes, they did. Many writers in the Old Testament would practically beg for help from God—and you can tell that what they really wanted was the close relationship with God. They didn't fully understand it, but what they wanted was the filling of the Holy Spirit.

Q: What was it like when the Holy Spirit came?

A: On the day of Pentecost, seven weeks after Jesus left his tomb, the believers were meeting together in one place. Suddenly a violent wind came from heaven, and—check this out!—tongues of fire settled on each of them as a physical indication of his presence. They were all filled with the Holy Spirit and began to speak in other languages as the Spirit enabled them. At this point Peter (otherwise known as the Rock) stood up and announced to the crowd, "*This* is what Joel, the prophet in the Old Testament, was talking about!"

Q: Now how can you tell that the Holy Spirit is around and working?

A: By the fruits of the Spirit. But we're not talking apples, peaches, and bananas. The fruits of the Spirit are love, joy, peace, patience, kindness, goodness, faithfulness, gentleness, and self-control. Just like the fruit we eat, the fruits of the Spirit are seen after something has taken root and started to grow. And you can let the Holy Spirit produce as much fruit as he wants because the Bible says that there is no law against these kinds of things.

Q: After the Holy Spirit fills us, does he leave and come back, or does he stay?

A: A: He stays. The Bible says that the body of a Christian is a "house" for the Holy Spirit. He moves in with you. Your body is one of his addresses. Sometimes the Holy Spirit is more noticeable—such as when he's convicting you or when he gives you an extra boost to do something challenging or when he's empowering you to do special things like prophesying—but most of the time he is just sitting there waiting for us to need him.

<FACTOID>

The Devil works like crazy to convince us that sin is not a problem. Part of the Holy Spirit's job is tell us "whoa, wait a minute" because sin separates us from God. And that *is* a problem. So when the Holy Spirit "convicts" us (makes sure we know that we've done wrong), he is actually doing us a big favor.

BeSiDeS THaT...

- Just like asking your friends to come over, you can invite the Holy Spirit to come over—except he never has to leave. A permanent sleepover. And you don't even have to ask your parents first.
- The Holy Spirit is a person. We have a relationship with him. With your friends you talk back and forth and enjoy each other's company. You can do the same with the Holy Spirit.
- He will fill you only as much as you allow him to. He won't bully his way in.
- The more you listen to the Holy Spirit, and let him control you, the more you will begin to experience the awesome power, the thrill, and the satisfaction of knowing God.
- The filling of the Spirit happens when we need it the most. The Holy Spirit fills us when we need the power and the guts to speak out about God. He fills us when we have a big problem to deal with. The Holy Spirit will even fill us just because we realize our need and ask him to.
- God does not limit how many times we can be filled. In fact, the Bible says we are to keep on being filled. Though it sometimes seems unlikely, it *is* possible to eat too much pizza—but it is *impossible* to get too full of the Holy Spirit.

What Difference Does It Make?

The difference between inviting the Spirit into your life and not inviting him is:

Being sealed or not being sealed into God's family.

Remember:

- On the package of every new Nintendo game, a seal indicates its authenticity—in other words, it's not an imitation or a copycat. It's the real deal. Certifiably so. This is what the Holy Spirit does with us. He puts his stamp of ownership on us. This seal is our proof positive that we are 100% pure Christian and that we belong to God.
- If anyone does not have the Holy Spirit in her, she doesn't belong to Jesus. But if someone is a Christian, the Holy Spirit does live in her. This is the seal that shows she belongs to God.
- This seal is not something you can see, like a tattoo that says, "Holy Spirit." It is an invisible seal. But God can see it, and people who hang out with you will see how it affects you.
- The Holy Spirit comes to live in you the instant you accept Jesus Christ—even though you still mess up sometimes.

(Scripture passages to support this chapter)

Believe It or Not

- The Holy Spirit prays for us—Romans 8:26

Zoom In

- The Holy Spirit gives gifts—1 Corinthians 12:8–10

CHapteR five

What event marked the greatest tragedy in the history of the human race?

HiNT

It involves a tree, a piece of fruit from that tree, a snake, and a fateful decision made by the first man and woman who ever walked the face of this earth. The end result of these four things altered human history and prompted God to send his Son Jesus down to earth.

Sin

What event marked the greatest tragedy in the history of the human race?

Adam and Eve's first home was a beautiful garden that God had made for them to live in. It was a spectacular world filled with many amazing creatures in a totally perfect habitat. The fish of the sea, the birds of the air, the animals, and all the bugs that crawl on the ground were given to Adam and Eve to care for and enjoy. They were given authority over these creatures and Adam was given the job of giving each one of them a name. ("Hey you over there with an extra tail in front—you'll be called an elephant!"). They were also the first people to become famous since they were the first people that God made. In the cool evenings, they walked and talked face-to-face with God. They could have lived happily ever after . . . if a tragic event hadn't changed all that.

Instead of listening to God, Eve listened to a snake—who was actually the Devil—and ate the fruit he gave her from the Tree of Knowledge. It was the one tree from which God said they could not eat. Well, that bite changed everything. Sin entered the world. Yucky, hideous, disgusting sin. Absolute filth. That event at the dawn of time is what we now call "the Fall."

Believe it oR NOt

God made you in his image.

The image of God that we are given is not the kind that you would see in a mirror or in a photo album of your last vacation, but it is a reflection of who God is. The image of God has to do with our spirit.

Adam and Eve actually talked face-to-face with God.

In the evenings, Adam and Eve walked with God in the garden. God gave them the ability to use their minds and enough intelligence to talk to him. They talked to God and God talked to them. This was not a long-distance phone call up to heaven—this was real, up-close, and personal time with God.

The first man was once dirt.

We were created very much on purpose. The same God who spoke the universe into existence created the first human being "out of the dust" of the earth.

God breathed his life into man.

We became human when God breathed the "breath of life" into this man made of dust. The man became a living, breathing being. This human being was also a very special creation that God created in "his own image."

The first woman was once a spare rib.

He then took a rib from this man (don't worry, Adam was sleeping), and out of that spare rib he created a woman. She was also created in the image of God.

That awful feeling when we know that we have done something wrong is a good thing.

It's called a conscience, and God built it into us for our own good.

Part 1

Because part of our humanity is God-breathed we are more than just a body made up of cells and DNA and flesh and bones. We have a soul and spirit, which is the part of us that we can't see. This part of you cannot be cloned, duplicated, or re-created. You are a one-of-a-kind, custom-built creation of God. Sometimes we call this part of us that we can't see our heart. But God sees us as one whole person with a body, soul, and spirit.

Part 2

Look at a pet dog or cat. Does it ever ask, "Is there a God?" Has it ever built a skyscraper or created a cool new music video? Of course not. They can be our buddies but they cannot create. We can do these things because we are different from the animals. We are God's special creation.

- Adam and Eve's disobedience brought sin to the entire human race.
- Sin ruined everything God had planned for his creation.
- Sin forces people to work hard to survive.
- Sin is now part of our nature.
- We have all sinned and are headed for certain death because of our sin. No exceptions.
- Sin separates us from God. It makes us very alone.
- Sin results in that horrible guilty feeling.
- Sin brings feelings of sadness.
- Sin distorts the image of God in us.
- Sin makes God very sad.
- All sin breaks God's law—whether it is a big sin or a little sin.
- All sin is directed against God. When we sin, even though it involves other people, God is the one we have sinned against.

God cannot and will not tolerate even the slightest speck of sin. Sin is ugly and disgusting to God. Imagine the grossest, most putrid thing on earth. That's what sin looks like to God. We can't always see sin, but God can.

- Without Jesus we'd be stuck with our sin.
- Jesus was God landing on earth. Jesus was one of us. Jesus is our passport for getting into heaven when we die.
- Jesus died on the cross to become the sacrifice that could pay for our sin—a once and for all sacrifice.
- Through Jesus, God forgives our sins.
- Because we've sinned, we deserve death. God's grace is what we get instead of what we deserve to get from God. Grace is when God gives us good things we don't deserve.
- When Jesus forgives our sins, we become new people. Our new selves begin to look like Jesus in his deeds and thoughts. This new self is in competition with the old self. We are headed towards a sin-free eternity; and when we get there, our old selves will be left far behind.
- All we have to do is choose to accept Jesus' forgiveness.

Q: How could Adam and Eve choose sin when sin hadn't entered the world yet?

A: Before sin came into the world, Adam and Eve just wanted to be with God. It was a part of their nature. They didn't want to sin. However, they were capable of being tempted and they were capable of making choices. Both Adam and Eve chose to sin when they were tempted to do so—that free-will thing at work.

Q: What would the world be like if Adam and Eve had not sinned?

A: If they had chosen not to sin, everything would be different. We'd all be living in the garden talking to God and nothing bad would ever happen. This is the world God wants to restore for us, and someday he will. But meanwhile, we are stuck with sin and all the nasty things it brings.

Q: If sin is so bad, and we are born with it, does that mean that we are awful people no matter what we do?

A: No. God didn't create awful people. God created us in his image and gave us life out of his breath. It's true that we are born wanting to sin, but good things come out of us because we are God's creation. God wants to get rid of the sin, not us. But because of sin, we are still separated from God—and that is a problem for us.

Q: Are you saying that even people like Billy Graham and Mother Teresa sin?

A: The nicest people sin. Some people sin more often than other people, and some people's sins cause more suffering than other people's, but sin is still sin. And we all do it.

Q: Aren't big sins, like murder, worse than little sins?

A: Clearly there is a difference between an ax murderer and someone who calls her little brother an idiot. And consequences to big sins are very serious. But, the little sins are still sinful. Two things remain true about sin, big or little: The first is that all sin is directed against God. The second is that we break God's law when we sin.

Q: Can you think of a way to help me understand that even little sins look bad to God?

A: Imagine sin as changes in elevation. Think of a person with very small sins on a sand dune at a beach. This person doesn't look so far off to us. Now imagine a person with a mountain of big sins on Mount Everest (29,000 feet above sea level). We see her as monstrously bad. It would seem that the person on Mount Everest doesn't have a chance at being good enough to meet God's standards while the person on the sand dune is a hair away from being good enough. Well, think about this from God's perspective: he has his standard, and he looks at us; only his view looks more like pictures taken from outer space. Sand dunes and Mount Everest look the same from up there.

BeSiDeS THaT...

Have you ever wondered what it would be like to have a robot around the house? It could do your chores for you and maybe your homework. It could even talk to you. All you'd have to do is to program it to do those things and teach it how to obey your commands.

But once your chores and your homework are done, you're bored.

So you think that maybe you'd like to have a friend over. But why call a friend when you've got your robot to keep you company? Easy answer: because a robot is boring to hang out with. A robot cannot choose to be your friend. All a robot can do is what it has been programmed to do.

God didn't want robots to keep him company; God wanted friends. That's why he created us as humans instead of robots.

Since he was God he could have forced us to love him, but he didn't. He wanted us to choose to love him. This choice he gave us is called free will.

God's gift of free will left Adam and Eve free to choose whether they would obey or disobey God. They chose to disobey, to sin. C. S. Lewis once said that God knew that would happen, but he thought it was worth the risk.

We're not robots. Our sinful choices have separated us from God.

<Factoid>

Just in case you're thinking that if you were in Adam's shoes you would not have sinned, think again. You probably don't have to think back very far to the last time that you sinned. That proves you would have sinned given the choice—because we all choose to sin repeatedly.

An apple tree is not an apple tree because it bears apples—it bears apples because it is an apple tree. We are not sinners because we sin—we sin because we are sinners. Got that? Sin can be tricky.

What Difference Does It Make?

The difference between forgiven sin and unforgiven sin is:

Eternal joy in heaven with God or eternal separation from God.

Remember:

- We are all born in sin. We all sin.
- Because Jesus died on the cross, he has the power to forgive our sin.
- If we want his forgiveness, we have to ask for it.
- When he forgives us, we receive eternal life.

Where Did You Find That?

(Scripture passages to support this chapter)

Zoom In

- We have all sinned—Romans 3:23
- Sin separates us from God—Isaiah 59:2
- God can't tolerate sin—Habakkuk 1:13

CHapteR six

Why does God allow suffering and evil?

HiNT

Evil hasn't always existed in our world. Back when humans were first created, nothing bad happened. God crafted a perfect world for humans. He gave us everything we could want or need—even free will.

SUFFERING & EVIL

Why does God allow suffering and evil?

God created a perfect world. He created a place with no evil in it. He also created humans and gave them the ability to make choices. This ability or freedom to do as we choose is called free will. But something terrible happened that changed everything. Adam and Eve chose to disobey God—to reject him. That choice was the first sin. Because of that sin, all the people that have come after them have been born as sinners. Sinners—not God—chose evil and caused suffering.

God is holy and hates evil. But he tolerates evil for now because he is waiting for more people to accept him. He wants everyone to spend eternity with him. When he finally does send Jesus back to earth to gather up his people to heaven, he will destroy evil forever.

Believe it OR NOt

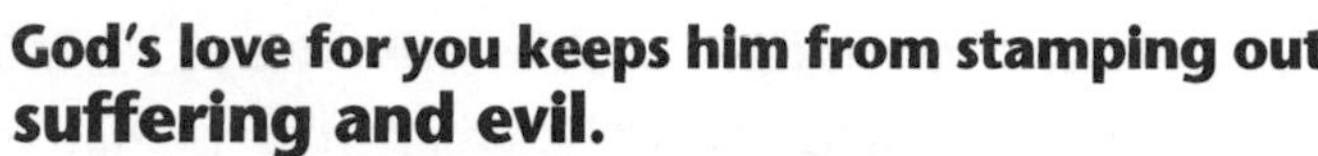

God's love for you keeps him from stamping out suffering and evil.

If God were to stamp out evil, he would do a complete job. He can't pick and choose and get rid of big things like war and hunger but not people who tell a lie or are mean to their classmates. Suppose God was to say, "Okay, at midnight tonight, all evil will be gone off the face of the earth?" Would we be waking up the next morning bright-eyed, cheery, and pouring our favorite cereal? No. We would be gone off the face of the earth and we wouldn't be having a very good day at all. God knows this and has decided not to stamp out evil. He wants all people to be saved.

Even though God hates sin, he loves sinful people.

God hates sin. Sin hurts us and we hurt each other because of sin. A time is coming when God will wipe all sin and evil off this planet. The problem is that we as human beings are sinful and he doesn't want to wipe us out—because he loves us. He sent Jesus to get rid of evil without getting rid of us.

The Devil is powerful enough to cause misery for the whole earth, but he has no power over us if we use Jesus' name.

Do you know what the Devil loves doing more than anything else? He just loves to wreck things. He's mad at God so he wants to ruin God's creation. He loves to cause suffering and misery; and God allows him to do this, for now. But God has given us the power through Jesus Christ to tell the Devil to go away and leave us alone.

God doesn't promise that life will always be fair.

The "exact reward concept," which means that you get exactly what's coming to you, doesn't necessarily work out here on earth. Sometimes people who are cruel and evil seem to escape punishment while people who do good things seem to suffer. God doesn't sit up in heaven and look at our deeds and then give us suffering or reward based on what we do, like he's keeping score. He has good reasons for everything.

Good can come out of bad.

Sometimes God allows suffering so that good things can come out of it. God doesn't expect us to understand, he just wants us to trust him. The New Testament says everything works out for the good of those who love him. In the Old Testament, Habakkuk said that he would rejoice in the Lord even though "there are no sheep in the pen and cattle in the stalls." You may not think that not having sheep or cows is suffering, but for this guy it was because they provided his food and clothing. He had faith that God was still good even though he might go hungry and be cold. Good things did happen for Habakkuk, just as they will for us when we trust God.

ZOOM iN

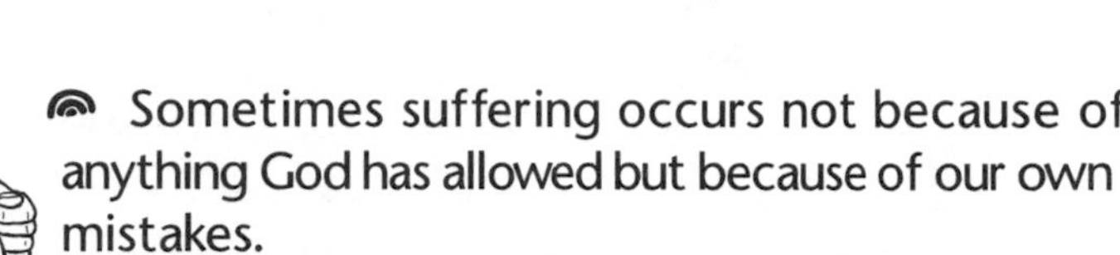

- Sometimes suffering occurs not because of anything God has allowed but because of our own mistakes.
- When a person drinks too much alcohol, drives, and causes an accident that kills someone, that person's actions caused the suffering. We can't blame God.
- Sometimes we suffer because of our own choices. If a kid gets grounded for disobeying, then that kid is suffering the consequences of his own disobedience.
- At times our own ignorance causes others to suffer. We may accidentally hurt someone's feelings by saying things that aren't true.
- Suffering can also come as a result of natural disasters—especially when people ignore warning signs.
- Sometimes God allows suffering as punishment in order to help people repent and turn from their sins. He wants them to learn from this punishment.
- God can transform any kind of suffering into good.
- Satan is the enemy of God. He gets his kicks from doing evil deeds and loves it when people suffer. He is nasty and mean and hates it when good things happen.

- Sometimes we (wrongly!) think of God up there somewhere—as if he sits on a cloud in a comfortable chair watching us down here suffering and thinks, *Oh well. Stuff happens.*
- God sees and cares about every single thing that happens to us.
- When we suffer, God suffers.
- He knows when we are hurt or in pain.
- He knows when we are sad or lonely. He *feels* it himself.
- The Bible says that Jesus was a "man of sorrows and familiar with suffering." The suffering Jesus lived through was greater than what any other human being has ever felt.
- Because Jesus suffered, he knows how we feel when we suffer.
- The next time you feel sad or are in pain remember that God is right there with you.

When God sent Jesus to die on the cross, he conquered sin, evil, and suffering for all of eternity.

It is not necessary for us to understand exactly why suffering exists. All we have to know is that God wants only good things for us.

Q: When will God finally destroy all suffering and evil?

A: He has to wait until the final judgment day, otherwise good could be destroyed along with evil. Until then, he has promised to be alongside us, helping us through times of suffering. You can count on this.

Q: If I could follow God perfectly, could I escape all suffering?

A: That's a big if. Not a day goes by that any of us can say that we have been perfect; besides, bad choices made by other people can also cause suffering. So the answer is no. But the Bible promises that evil and suffering will one day be stamped out forever!

Q: If God were really fair, wouldn't he make the bad people suffer and allow all the good people to be happy?

A: The problem with this idea is that nobody is good. Jesus said that only God is good. If God judged us exactly according to our behavior we would be doomed. When we are honest with ourselves, we should be thankful that God is being so patient.

Q: Does God help us when we suffer?

A: He sure does. When we trust God, he helps us feel joy in the midst of suffering. Sometimes he uses our pain to make us better people. Though suffering comes as a result of sin, we are not doomed to a life of suffering when we walk with God.

BeSiDeS THaT...

- God's chosen people, the Israelites, behaved just the way we do and suffered just the way we do.
- God didn't want his chosen people to suffer, so he often warned them of trouble.
- He told them flat out what was going to happen if they turned away from him. He sent prophets to beg them to listen. He did everything he could to get their attention.
- Sometimes they would repent and obey God for a while. But pretty soon they would lapse back into temporary amnesia and forget everything God had said.
- God would have to get their attention all over again. This pattern went on pretty much all the way through the whole Old Testament.
- Eventually God had to judge them for their disobedience. God himself had to make them suffer.

<FacToiD>

God never wants to punish. That's why he gives lots of warnings and lots of opportunities for people to come to him. The Bible says that he "takes no pleasure in the death of the wicked" and that he tells us to "turn from your evil ways." He sent Jesus into the world so that we could be saved from death.

Some people say, "If God is so good and loves everyone so much, why would he send anyone to hell?" Actually, God doesn't send anyone to hell; we send ourselves to hell when we choose not to accept God's solution for sin, which is Jesus. God gives us every opportunity *not* to go to hell.

What Difference Does It Make?

The difference between trusting God (even when we see so much suffering) and not trusting God (because the suffering confuses us) is:

Living joyfully under God's good and perfect plan or living in despair.

Remember:

- Suffering can make you more like Jesus.
- Suffering can turn into joy.
- Suffering can help us become better people.

WHeRe DiD YOU FiND THaT?

(Scripture passages to support this chapter)

Believe It or Not

- God doesn't stamp out evil because he wants everyone to come to repentance—2 Peter 3:9
- God works through suffering to produce good—Romans 8:28
- God cares about everything that happens to us—Matthew 10:29–31

Some people believe happiness should be our goal in life. But true happiness does not come from having all the things that you want or from having lots of friends or even being rich or famous. Many, many people who have everything they have ever dreamed of are still miserable. Only God can make us truly happy.

When we blame God for bad things, we are saying one of the following sentences is true:

- God is all-powerful but not all good; he doesn't want to stop evil.
- God is completely good but unable to stop evil; he is not all-powerful.

The truth is, both statements are wrong. God is not to blame for bad things.

Rewind

Chapter 4

- Jesus sent the Holy Spirit to earth at Pentecost.
- The Holy Spirit comforts us, convicts us, leads us to truth, and gives us gifts.
- The Holy Spirit is an invisible seal proving we belong to Christ. He lives inside every Christian.

Chapter 5

- Sin first entered the world when Adam and Eve disobeyed God. Since then, everyone has been born with a sinful nature.
- Sin separates us from God, but Jesus' death on the cross became the sacrifice that allows God to forgive us. We can enjoy a relationship with him.
- When you ask God to forgive your sins, he makes you into a new person.

Chapter 6

- Satan is the cause of evil in the world.
- Because God loves us, when we suffer, he suffers, too.
- God can work good through anything, even suffering and evil.
- At the end of time, God will finally get rid of Satan and stamp out all suffering and evil.

Chapter seven

What gift is more valuable than gold or diamonds, yet has been rejected by billions of people?

HiNT

It isn't in a box wrapped in paper and tied with a big bow, like a Christmas present or a birthday present. It's more like it's sitting on a shelf at the store with a big tag on it that says, "Take one; it's FREE."

Once we accept it, this gift is ours to keep. It is available to every human being who has ever existed and who ever will exist. It cost the Giver a lot, but it is free to us. And even though we don't have to accept this gift, God offers it to us anyway.

Salvation

What gift is more valuable than gold or diamonds, yet has been rejected by billions of people?

Salvation. It's free to us because it cost Jesus so much. He gave his life to pay for it.

Believe it OR NOt

Sometimes, seemingly smart people do dumb things—like turning down the world's best gift.

You know how near the end of a movie it always looks as if bad guys have won and the good guys are about to be dropped into a burning pit of acid? And then . . . the hero rushes in and saves the good guys just in the nick of time? It's like that with Jesus. We are about to be dropped into a burning pit, and Jesus rushes in to save us. Except first he stops and asks, "Do you want to be saved?" At this point I don't know why anyone would say no, but people do. Even though the Bible makes it clear that if we reject God, we accept death.

God lets us choose where we want to spend eternity.

Sin brings certain death and eternal damnation, which is hell. Jesus saves us from all that and gives us the much more pleasant option of living with God up in heaven for all of eternity—all that's required of us is to say, "Yes, I want that." This is salvation. It's totally up to us to pick our eternal destination. God gave us free will and so we need to make our own decision. Not even our parents can decide that for us. One thing is certain: We deserve death and will receive death *unless* we ask Jesus to save us.

John the Baptist ate locusts and shouted stuff about his cousin, Jesus.

Six months before Jesus' birth, his cousin John was born. When John grew up, people nicknamed him John the Baptist because he went around baptizing people. An odd sort of fellow, he spent a lot of time wandering around the wilderness eating locusts with honey on them and continually shouting, "REPENT! The kingdom of heaven is coming!" He was talking about Jesus, of course. Many people believed John, but many didn't. He made the wife of King Herod so mad she asked her husband to chop his head off. And Herod did it because he didn't want his wife mad at him. After his cousin died, Jesus told people to repent.

ZOOM IN

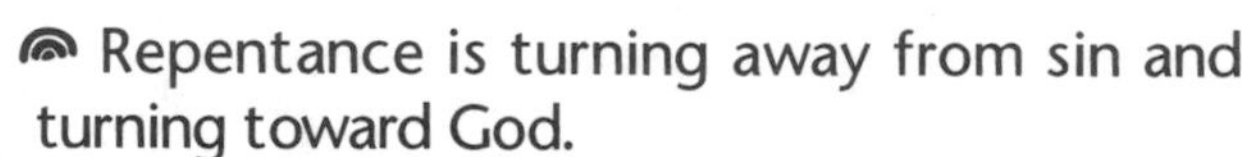

- Repentance is turning away from sin and turning toward God.
- Repentance is not just *feeling* sorry for your sins, not just *knowing* that you are a sinner, and not just *deciding* not to sin anymore. It is all three of these put together.
- To become a Christian, you must repent. You must believe that Jesus is the Son of God, he died to save you from your sins, and he came alive again. You need to know him. It's not enough to believe these things *might* be true. You can't think maybe *some* of them are true. You must believe every one of them to be true. It's an all or nothing kind of a deal.
- You need to make a decision to *keep on* believing. It just doesn't make sense to say, "Okay, it's true"—and then walk away. You will continue to need Jesus.
- You have to stick with Jesus even when you might not feel like it.
- When you decide to become a Christian, you don't need to worry about doing it right or saying it wrong. God knows your heart and he knows your intentions better than you do.
- As you step toward God, he comes running to you, grabs you by the hand, and shows you what you need to know and do. And then all the angels in heaven have a huge party.
- Your faith (having confidence in something) brings you to God, and God helps your faith to grow, which brings you to closer to God, and allows him to help your faith to grow more, which brings you to closer to God. . . . See a pattern here?

- You will begin to see the work of the Holy Spirit in your life. Remember when we talked about fruit that came not from the grocery store but from the Holy Spirit working in our lives? Start looking and you might just find some of that good fruit. Maybe it's something small like being nice to someone that you might have ignored before, or something big like deciding that it's not such a good idea to rob that bank after all.

ZOOM OUT

- Jesus told this guy Nicodemus, who asked Jesus point-blank what he needed to do to be saved, that he needed to be born again. Jesus wasn't talking about second physical birth from a mother (trust me, your mother wouldn't be too pleased at the whole idea!), but a spiritual birth involving the non-physical parts of you.
- Rebirth is necessary because we are sinful. The old self dies, and the new self is born.
- When someone becomes a Christian, from that instant forward she is a new person.

OLD SELF: I want it my way and I want it now.

NEW SELF: I want to do it God's way and I plan to start now.

OLD SELF: Whatever makes me happy is what I'll do.

NEW SELF: How can I make God happy?

OLD SELF: Yo! I'm pretty cool.

NEW SELF: Actually, upon further examination, I'm not always all that cool.

OLD SELF: I'm not very good at anything, and I don't look like Brittany Spears.

NEW SELF: Hey! I'm made in the image of God, how cool is that?

OLD SELF: Slow train to hell.

NEW SELF: Destination heaven.

We continue changing until we receive our brand-new and improved bodies in heaven.

True repentance automatically sends you on your way to faith.

Faith is believing in and being sure about something you can't see. Have you learned what an "object of a preposition" is? Well, Jesus is the object of our faith. No other object is worth our time.

Q: What can I do to earn salvation?

A: Absolutely, positively NOTHING. Salvation is a free gift. You cannot get it by working extra hard, by doing good deeds, or by staying out of trouble. It is grace (the willingness of God to save us when we don't deserve it) that saves us—not good deeds. When you receive salvation you will want to do good things to help others and to please God, but trying to earn your way into heaven is impossible.

Q: What's the difference between regular Christians and born-again Christians?

A: Not really anything. All true Christians are born again. Sometimes people use the term "born again" to make a point about the difference between people who think they are Christians just because they go to church on Sundays and people who know they are Christians because they are saved.

Q: What does the word justification mean?

A: Making things right. Think about this: God set up his law, and we have all broken it. Because we have broken the law, God must judge us. The punishment for breaking God's law requires the death penalty. God the Judge says, "Okay, I'll substitute the death of Jesus for the death that all human beings deserve." Our defense when facing the death penalty is that our sin has been justified by what Jesus did. Our sins have been erased forever. Deleted. Without a trace.

Q: What is salvation?

A: When Jesus died on the cross he took care of all your sins for all of time. He doesn't have to keep dying over and over again. And you don't have to worry about having to pay for your sins when you meet God. Unfortunately, you will continue to sin as long as you live in your earthly body, but as long as you are sorry, God will continue to forgive you. In a sense you have the receipt that says "bought and paid for." You are saved. And no one can take this away from you.

Q: What is sanctification?

A: Sanctification means God is making you more like Jesus every day. Once you are saved, you start the process of sanctification. You are on the road to becoming holy and righteous. The more you learn about your own sin the more you see your need for God's help. The more you see your need for God's help, the more he helps you. You are learning to be holy, even though sometimes it seems that you are not going anywhere.

Q: What is glorification?

A: In the end, you will be saved, holy, righteous, and sin-free. This is called glorification. When you die you will have a big 'SAVED' stamped on your forehead. Well, not really, but think of it as an imaginary stamp that automatically sends you catapulting into glory when you die. You already have justification for your sins through Jesus, you've been headed for glory all along through sanctification, and now you've arrived at your eternal glorification destination all justified and sanctified. Cool. So take these three things, and put them in your pocket; take them out when you need a reminder (pretty much all the time), and remember that Jesus is your Savior.

BeSiDeS THaT...

- It's not God's fault if all people don't get saved. No one in hell will be able to truthfully claim she wanted to be saved but God didn't pick her.
- The Bible is clear that *all* are welcome to accept his free gift of salvation. If you want to be saved and you ask God to save you—then you are saved. This is all you need to know.
- The word *election* means that God chooses whom he wants to receive salvation; but since he offers it to everyone, then it is clear he has chosen everyone.
- *Predestination* means that before we were born we had a date with destiny to become a Christian.
- *Foreknowledge* means God knew ahead of time who would choose him. It is good to know God thought about us before time began, and he thought of salvation before we even knew we needed it. What an awesome God!
- People who have never read the Bible still have no excuse not to know God. The book of Romans says they have seen the earth and sky and God has shown them his invisible qualities all their lives.

What Difference Does It Make?

The difference between accepting God's offer of salvation and rejecting it is:

Eternal joy in heaven or eternal misery in hell.

Remember:

- Since God cannot lie, you can believe everything he says about salvation.
- Jesus paid a high price so he could offer us the free gift of salvation.
- Anyone who wants salvation can have it.
- Accepting the gift of salvation is the only way to heaven.

(Scripture passages to support this chapter)

Zoom Out

- A new Christian is a "new person"—2 Corinthians 5:17

Ask Professor Little

- We can't earn salvation—Ephesians 2:8–9

Besides That . . .

- All are welcome to accept salvation—John 3:16
- Everyone can know about God's power, even if he hasn't read the Bible—Romans 1:20

CHapteR

eight

Are miracles really possible?

HiNT

Could a big fish really swallow Jonah and then spit him out alive? (Kinda gross, huh?) Do you *really* think that Jesus fed five thousand people with five loaves of bread and only two fish?

You are old enough to know that miracles are not possible by ordinary human beings acting on their own. The fat man in the red suit who supposedly squeezes down your chimney and then floats back up and flies through the sky with reindeer (wouldn't a plane make more sense?) can't really do any of those things. In order to perform miracles, superhuman beings, like a Pokemon, need supernatural powers. The problem is, they are fictional and their powers are limited by whoever imagined them.

A real miracle requires the power of a being who actually exists, is all-powerful, and who has the authority to make things happen.

Miracles

Are miracles really possible?

Since God exists, is all-powerful, and has ultimate authority, we can say, yes, miracles are possible.

Believe it OR NOt

Some people call coincidences "miracles."

Sometimes people use the word miracle to mean something that is unusual or unexpected. If there is a fire drill at the very moment your teacher starts giving a spelling test you might say, "It's a miracle!" This is not really a miracle (but you might be thanking God, anyway). It is just a fire drill at a very choice moment.

God never tries to impress anyone, but he impresses people anyway.

The miracles in the Bible always occurred for a reason. God would never have said, "Oh, what the hey, I think I'll do a little miracle. They could use some entertainment down there." Each miracle was intended to help people have faith in God or to meet their needs.

The Devil tried to goad Jesus into getting something for himself.

Jesus also performed miracles with a purpose in mind. He never performed a miracle to "show off." He never performed miracles to get something for himself. The Devil tried to talk Jesus into performing miracles to "prove" himself, but Jesus refused. He said what everyone should say to the Devil when we're asked us to do things that we are not supposed to. Jesus just said, "No." And if the Devil doesn't like that answer, you can say: "What part of 'no' don't you understand?"

When you interrupt, you might be called rude. When God interrupts, we call it a miracle.

Miracles, as recorded in the Bible, are acts of God. An act of God occurs when God intentionally breaks into, changes, or interrupts what normally would have happened.

God doesn't have to obey the law.

Since God designed the universe, he certainly has the right to do with it what he wants. No matter what he does, he isn't breaking any natural laws because he is outside, over, and above natural law—not bound by it. He is free to do miracles until the cows come home (since he made them, too).

<Factoid>

Famous author G. K. Chesterton said, "A miracle is startling; but it is simple. It is simple because it is a miracle. It is power coming directly from God instead of indirectly from nature or human wills."

- Jesus' miracles were done in public. They were not performed in secret before only one or two people who then announced them to the world. They were performed in the open for all to see.
- Not everyone watching believed Jesus was the Son of God. Jesus was a skeptic-magnet. When Jesus performed miracles, lots of skeptics (people who are not yet sure) watched.
- Even the people who hated Jesus never denied his miracles, they just said the miracles came from evil powers. They felt very threatened by Jesus.
- The miracles of Jesus were real. He didn't just repeat the same miracle over and over; and he didn't do his miracles all at once, like the grand finale at a fireworks show. He exercised power over nature when he changed water into wine at a wedding. He demonstrated his power over disease when he healed sick people. He bossed demons around. He fed five thousand people from a couple of fish and a few loaves of bread. He told a storm to "cut that out" and it obeyed. And if all that's not enough, he proved his power over death when he brought a man named Lazarus back to life after he had been dead for four days. (Just in case you might be skeptical about this one, we know from the Bible that Lazarus had been dead for four days because his sister told Jesus that the body "stinks." True story.)
- After people who were disabled or sick were healed by Jesus, they were no longer skeptics. All the lepers and blind men Jesus healed believed in him. Talk about eyewitnesses!

- Some people think each miracle has a natural explanation. For instance, when God made the Red Sea split apart so the Israelites could escape from the Egyptians, some people think a very high wind caused the waters to part. Though unlikely, let's imagine that is the true explanation. Big deal. It's still a miracle. The high winds would have had to come just when the Israelites reached the shore and the Egyptians closed in on them in hot pursuit. Then after every Israelite safely reached the other side, the wind would have had to die down at exactly the right instant to prevent the Egyptians from catching them. Wow.
- Some miracles have no possible natural explanation. The best examples of this are the resurrections of Lazarus and of Jesus. The best doctors in the world cannot bring somebody back from the dead. Only God can do that. It would take a miracle.
- Skeptics say that the people Jesus healed weren't really sick, that they were faking it or just thought they were sick. But the people who were healed had sicknesses everyone could see, like leprosy. Leprosy is a disease that causes sores all over the body and never goes away. It is so bad that, in Bible times, lepers were cast out from society and forced to go live with other lepers. They could never go home. These people could not have been faking it.
- Skeptics claim that people in ancient times were stupid. They say the people simply didn't understand what was happening. What an insult! Of course the people knew what was possible and impossible. When a paralyzed man had to be carried to a house where Jesus taught, it didn't take a genius to recognize the miracle when the man stood up and walked out of the place. When Jesus gave sight to a man that had been blind from birth, the people who knew the healed guy knew that this miracle stuff was no joke. These were bona fide miracles!

Q: Why doesn't God do miracles now so that everyone will believe in him?

A: Jesus answered this question for us. He said: Once upon time, a rich man died and went to hell. The man looked to heaven, saw Abraham, and begged him to send someone to warn his brothers about the torments of hell so they wouldn't end up there. Abraham told the man his brothers already had all the information they needed in the Word of God. The rich man responded, "Yeah, I know, but maybe if they saw a miracle like someone being raised from the dead or something, *then* they would believe." The reply from heaven was, "Sorry, but if they won't listen to the Word of God, even the miracle of someone rising from the dead won't make a difference."

Q: Why did God perform miracles for the people back in the Bible and not for us?

A: Maybe we don't see as many miracles today because when he does we just explain them away with scientific theory. One thing is sure though: When God performs miracles, he does it for his good reasons, not for our entertainment.

Q: Are there miracles that aren't from God?

A: Yes. Miracles can come from demons. That's one reason the Bible tells us to test the spirits. Jesus said that in the last days there will be miracles so great that even Christians will be deceived if they aren't careful.

Q: Do you think science teachers should teach about miracles?

A: No, miracles are not a question for science teachers. (Although, if they are Christians they will believe in miracles.) Science, by its own definition, looks only at natural laws and not supernatural laws.

Q: Should any subject teach about miracles?

A: Philosophy, because philosophy studies truth. Philosophers are able to understand the concept of miracles because once they understand truth, they can understand what is possible with God. A true student of philosophy will eventually run into Jesus and will have to decide whether or not to accept him. (Note: Philosophy isn't usually taught until college.)

"I Doubt It" Dude meets "Is Too" Dude

"I Doubt It"

"The followers of Jesus must have been exaggerating when they talked of the miracles that Jesus performed. I mean, *come on*, everyone likes to make things sound more interesting than how it really happened. Right?"

"Is Too"

"Yeah, could be. But when we are looking for the truth about something that happened we ask someone who saw it with his very own eyeballs, an *eye*witness. If he is a trustworthy person we believe him."

Is there any evidence that these people couldn't be trusted?

"The followers of Jesus were his friends so, of course, they're going to say he performed miracles. I mean, duuuh!"

"First, it wasn't just his friends who saw the miracles. Also, just because they were friends of Jesus and believed in him doesn't mean they were liars. They were there, saw what they saw, and told people about it. Besides, they could have gotten into a lot of trouble for saying stuff like that, arrested and killed even. Why would they take that risk for a lie? They said Jesus performed miracles and I believe them."

What Difference Does It Make?

The difference between knowing and not knowing that all things are possible with God is:

Realizing that God can change our lives or being doomed to a life that is limited to what we can do for ourselves.

Remember:

- Only an all-powerful God has the power to perform miracles.
- When Jesus performed miracles he proved he was God.
- All God's miracles were for our benefit.

Chapter nine

Do angels, Satan, and demons really exist?

HiNT

We see angels everywhere: on the popular television show *Touched by an Angel*, in costumes and atop trees at Christmas, and in many movies that you can pick up at your local video store. The Devil and his demons are featured on boxes of Red Hots candy, in thriller movies, and for Halloween. These depictions are obviously make-believe. But where do these ideas come from?

Angels, Satan, and Demons

Do angels, Satan, and demons really exist?

The short answer is yes.

Believe it OR NOt

Even if we could see angels, we could never count them.

In a vision, Daniel saw thousands and thousands of angels and another ten thousand times ten thousand angels. That's an angel convention of astronomical proportions! Imagine a thousand sports arenas crammed with angels. The book of Revelation says that God's Spirit showed John at least as many angels as Daniel saw. Now I don't know if these were the same angels that appeared in Daniel's dream or different angels, but either way there are tons of angels whether you count them once or twice.

Michael Jordan is no angel, but there is an angel named Michael.

The Bible mentions the names of only two angels out of the thousands times ten thousand angels . . . and still counting. One was Michael, the other Gabriel. Michael was a warrior. He led a battle in heaven against none other than the devil himself. He also fought with the devil for the body of Moses. As if this wasn't enough, Michael's special mission was to watch over Israel and be one of its chief princes.

Gabriel blows his horn.

Gabriel, on the other hand, is famous for blowing his horn. This may not sound as exciting as Michael's job, but he gets to blow his horn and announce Jesus' return, which will be the most important moment in the entire history of the world. Except, of course, when Jesus came the first time. Which brings us to Gabriel's other claim to fame. He announced the births of John the Baptist *and* Jesus.

Angels might not have wings.

Contrary to popular opinion, no evidence proves that angels have wings. For some reason whenever people have decided to paint angels or describe them in books and stories they give them wings. Maybe this is because people thought that since they seem to get around so much in the Bible they would need a mode of transportation. Obviously they wouldn't have had sports cars or private jets to zoom around in when the Bible was being written so they were given wings by the artists who painted and drew them so they could fly around on their own.

Angels are heavenly beings created by God. In Greek, the word angel means messenger.

Cherubim have wings, but they may not be angels.

Two winged cherubim guarded the east entrance of the Garden of Eden with their not-so-ordinary flaming swords. Ezekiel describes cherubim as living creatures having, get this, four faces. Yes, you read that correctly, *four* faces—the face of a man, the face of a lion, the face of an ox, and the face of an eagle. They also have four wings. Two stretch upward, and the other two stretch downward covering their bodies. Pretty wild, huh?

Seraphim have six wings—and they're not insects.

Not to be outdone by the cherubim are the seraphim with their *six* wings. And they can fly. They have only one head, and they look human (which isn't a bad way to look). When the Bible mentions seraphim, they're usually guarding something which, given their appearance, is something they are well suited for.

- Angels are beings created by God. The Bible says everything in heaven and on earth, both visible and invisible, was created by God because he wanted to create them.
- Angels were around before God created Adam and Eve.
- Sometimes angels take on human form when they appear to people. The Bible says that some people (maybe you) have entertained angels as guests and didn't even know it. This might be a good reason to keep your room clean.
- Humans are special because we are created in the image of God. Angels aren't.
- Angels aren't male or female. They don't marry and have kids.
- Angels never die. They don't get old and wrinkled either.
- Someday we will have authority over the angels. Not a chance here on earth, though, because we are stuck in our sinful bodies. But one day, once we die and go to live in heaven with Jesus in our new and improved bodies, we will judge angels.
- Angels, even though they are hanging around up in the heavens with Jesus, don't know when Jesus will return to earth for us.
- Angels are dying to understand salvation. (Well, actually, they don't die so I guess that they aren't exactly dying to know; but they really, *really* do want to know.) But they can't. We, however, do get to understand salvation because we experience it. Wow! How cool is that?

- Angels have superhuman strength. One angel killed 185,000 Assyrians in one night. Not even all the superheroes combined can do that in a month's worth of Saturday morning cartoons. Angel power comes from God, though, and he told the angel to kill the wicked Assyrians so they couldn't hurt his chosen people.

- Angels see God face to face and worship him constantly. Jesus himself said this.
- Every time anyone on earth repents and decides to become a Christian, the angels throw a party and rejoice. They are aware of each of us, you and me included. (Have they had your party yet?)
- One angel-job is delivering news from God.
- Apparently angels are important to God because the Bible mentions them more than 250 times.
- Although many people believe guardian angels are on earth to protect us, the Bible does not say this specifically. However, the Bible does say children have angels in heaven watching out for them. Jesus himself said this to some adults who gathered around him one day.

- Angels are beings that exist for God's purposes. They are *not* to be worshiped.
- Angels clamped the mouths of hungry lions shut when Daniel was dropped into a pit full of the beasts. He was supposed to be their dinner. (Ouch!)
- One day Elijah ran into the desert to escape an evil ruler who wanted him dead. Angels brought the prophet freshly cooked bread and a jar of water . . . and he felt much better.
- When a ruler stuck Peter in jail for telling people about Jesus, angels came and sprung him out of jail—not once but twice. He had chains on and everything.
- An angel visited Paul on a ship in the middle of a huge storm. The angel said that Paul and all the others on board would survive, and they did. (They were survivors long before anyone ever thought of the TV show.)
- Angels visited Jesus on the night before his death to give him strength.
- When a lonely, homeless person in the Bible died, angels carried him up to heaven.
- When Jesus returns in "clouds of glory" *all* the angels will be surrounding him as he sits on a throne in heavenly glory. Cool.

Because Everyone Likes a True Story . . .

Throughout recent history, many people claim to have seen angels. Some of their claims we know to be false because their descriptions do not match what we know to be true about angels in the Bible. Others cannot be dismissed so quickly. One trustworthy account comes from a well-known missionary in a faraway land. His name is Paton. Here is his story:

Because of his success in spreading the Gospel, Paton had aroused the hatred of the local native chief. The chief hired someone to kill Paton. The hired killer went to the missionary's house, but instead of coming back to report the murder to the chief, the hit man returned in terror, saying he had seen a row of men, dressed in white, surrounding the missionary's home. The chief thought the man had drunk too much whiskey and encouraged him to try again. The next time others of the tribe accompanied him. That night they all saw three rows of men surrounding Paton's home. Later, when the chief asked Paton where he kept the guards who surrounded his house at night, Paton, knowing nothing of what had happened, disclaimed the whole idea. When the chief, in amazement, told his story, the missionary realized the natives had seen an angelic company, which God had sent to protect him.

No bodyguards . . .

Angels hang around God all the time, but that doesn't mean they stand between God and us like bodyguards. No. Never. We can talk to God anytime we want because of Jesus.

It is true, the Devil has a lot of power and only one mission: to destroy all that is good by any means possible. Not to worry. You have the Ultimate-Most-Extreme-Power with the Holy Spirit in you. All you need to do is speak the name of Jesus. That name will instantly turn the Devil and all his demons into whimpering cowards. They'll turn and run away so fast they will be a distant bumbling blur within milliseconds.

Q: Are demons worse than the bad guys in movies?

A: Much worse. Demons are fallen angels who hang out with the Devil. They are his personal servants. He sends them out to do his dirty work. One of the things demons did in the Bible was enter people's bodies and wreak all kinds of havoc. This is called demon possession. When demons entered bodies, they made some people sick and caused others to rant and rave like crazed lunatics.

Q: Are mentally ill people demon possessed?

A: It is important to realize that just because someone is sick or crazy it doesn't mean he is demon possessed. It just so happens that when the demons would possess someone that is how that person would look or act.

Q: Were there more demon-possessed people back in Jesus' time than there are today?

A: We have no way to know for sure, but demon possession seemed to be common in Jesus' time. Demon possession is rarely mentioned in the Old Testament or in the New Testament after Jesus went back to heaven. Maybe the Devil was especially furious because he knew Jesus had a plan to take care of our sin. Satan knew Jesus would put him out of business, so he caused as much trouble as possible. Kind of a last-ditch effort. He knew he was smoked.

Q: Are demons still around?

A: Demons still exist. Because of this it is very important to not fool around with things associated with the Devil like Ouija board games or occult (Devil worship) practices. Those are the kinds of things and places where the Devil and his demons might be slinking around.

Q: Does the Devil reward the demons for serving him?

A: Demons will get nothing for serving the Devil except a one-way ticket to the depths of a fiery pit in hell. Doesn't sound very appealing, does it? But that's reality when the Devil is your boss.

Q: Is it okay to call the Devil bad names?

A: The Bible often refers to the Devil as "the Evil One," "the Father of Lies," "the Tempter," "Supreme Deceiver," "a murderer," and "wicked." And that's just for starters. It is certainly okay for you to refer to him in any of those ways. He is also called Satan. He is the enemy of God and all that is good. There is nothing good about the Devil. He is always up to no good. Avoid him like the plague. He's bad to the bone. Leave him alone.

Satan's power over you is extremely limited

Satan's power is not as strong as God's power

Satan has to ask God before he can touch you

Satan doesn't know everything

Satan's headed for a lake of burning sulfur at the final judgment of God

BeSiDeS THaT...

- God has all the power and all the authority over the Devil.
- Since God is our friend and is on our side we have nothing to fear from the Devil.
- God created the Devil as a beautiful angel, but pride changed him. He talked other angels into rebelling against God and got kicked out of heaven. Ever since then, the Devil has been trying to get even by warring with God.
- He appeared as a snake in the Garden of Eden and introduced Adam and Eve to sin by lying to them. He had to lie because if he told the truth then they wouldn't have listened to him.
- Jesus made the Devil *really* mad when he died on the cross. The Devil knows he lost even though it seemed as if he had won.

- The Devil works hard at winning you and me away from God. He wants to cause God pain.
- We don't have to let him. We apply sunscreen so our skin won't look like a boiled lobster, and we use insect repellent to keep away mosquitoes. We can use the following Devil repellent to keep him away from us. We'll need:

  Plenty of face time with God—pray every day.

  A well-read Bible—wear those pages out.

  Solid faith—know your stuff and trust God.

- To defeat the Devil, put on God's armor. . .

  The belt of Truth (knowing what God is like)

  The breastplate of Righteousness (being squared away with Jesus)

  The shield of Faith (trusting God to keep his promises)

  The helmet of Salvation (knowing that you'll go to heaven someday)

  The sword of the Spirit (letting the Holy Spirit live in you)

  The shoes of Peace (always ready)

<Factoid>

How come the Devil is always shown wearing red, with horns, and carrying a pitchfork? Actually, I don't know. The Bible certainly doesn't describe him that way. Maybe the Devil himself wants people to think he is harmless so he can trick them into doing what he wants. He has even gone so far as to appear as an angel.

What Difference Does It Make?

The difference between believing and not believing in spiritual beings is:

Being aware and better prepared for or being unaware and unprepared for the spiritual battle happening right now for your soul.

Remember:

- The Devil is determined to "get" you.
- The Devil has no power over you when you speak Jesus' name against him.
- A good defense against the Devil is knowing what the Bible says and spending lots of time in prayer.
- Don't spend your time thinking about the Devil. Keep your mind on God.

(Scripture passages to support this chapter)

Zoom In

- You might have entertained an angel—Hebrews 13:2
- Angels don't get married—Luke 20:35–36

Zoom Out

- Angels rejoice when people are saved—Luke 15:10

Besides That . . .

- Put on the armor of God—Ephesians 6:10–18

Factoid

- Satan has to ask God before he touches you—Job 1:9–12; 2:4–6

What Difference Does It Make?

- We can resist Satan—James 4:7

REWIND

Chapter 7

- Salvation is free. We can do nothing to earn it, but we do have to ask for it.
- Repentance is knowing you are a sinner, feeling sorry for your sins, and deciding not to sin anymore.
- To become a Christian, you must repent, ask God to forgive you, and believe Jesus is the Son of God who died for your sins.

Chapter 8

- Miracles occur when God intentionally changes or interrupts normal events.
- God allowed some people in the Old and New Testaments to perform miracles.
- Jesus performed many miracles, and even the people who hated him never denied them.

Chapter 9

- Angels are heavenly spirit beings created by God. They are mentioned more than 250 times in the Bible, but they should never be worshiped.
- Sometimes angels take on human form and appear to people.
- Every time anyone on earth repents and becomes a Christian, the angels throw a party and rejoice.
- God has all power and all authority over the Devil. You need never fear him.

CHapteR ten

When will Jesus return?

One of the most fascinating things about the Bible is that it tells us what lies ahead for our world. Both the Old and New Testament say that someday the world will end, but that's okay because God is in control. He has been all along. Throughout the Old Testament, the prophets looked forward to the "Day of the Lord" when God would finally get his world back from sin. For all of those who know and love God, it will be a great day. For those who chose not to know and love God it will be a terrible day.

THINGS TO COME

When will Jesus return?

We don't know. Only God knows the answer to that question.

Believe it OR NOt

Predictions in the Bible come true 100% of the time.

Throughout the Bible, predictions are made about things to come. And they *always* come true. They aren't like the predictions psychics make on television or at a carnival or like a horoscope in the newspaper. (By the way, those kinds of predictions are not from God and Christians aren't supposed to listen to them.) The predictions in the Bible come from God and have more than one purpose. Sometimes they warn us so we can turn to God and start making good decisions. Other times they give us hope of sensational things to come so we have something to look forward to. One of the major reasons God predicts events in advance is to assure us that everything the Bible says is true. After the event, people can slap their foreheads and say, "Oh! *That's* what God meant! It happened exactly as he said it would."

The predictions God gave us are like a puzzle we can try to figure out.

The Bible mentions several events that will happen before Jesus returns. Because these are often hard to understand, even Christians who study the Bible have different opinions on when and how they will occur. However, all Christians agree that they will occur.

It'll be on a Tuesday, at approximately 1:52 p.m., Mountain Standard Time—NOT!

We should live each day wondering if today is the day we will see Jesus. But since God didn't want us to know the precise time, people who spend time trying to figure out the *exact* day and time that Jesus is coming back are foolish and, quite frankly, wasting their time. We do need to keep watching for his coming, but we won't need binoculars or a special news alert on the radio, because when he returns the whole world will know. Big time!

You will want to avoid the Tribulation if at all possible.

The Tribulation will be a period of time when the Devil gets to have his way here on earth. The Antichrist (anti = against) will be an evil leader with supernatural powers given to him by the Devil. At first he might be seen as an exciting new leader who claims to worship God, but Christians will know differently. He will have political power and the ability to control what we buy and sell. Terrible consequences will be given to those of us who refuse to follow him.

Christians from every place on earth and from all time will witness Christ's second coming.

When Jesus disappeared behind a cloud as he left earth the first time, two men dressed in white (Do you think they were angels?) told the disciples he'd come back the same way he left. *Except*, the Bible tells us later that when Jesus comes back to get us, there will be more than two angels with him. All the believers who have died will be resurrected, and together with all the believers that are still living, they will meet Jesus in the clouds. It will be so spectacular, so outrageous, so incredibly fantastic, so completely awesome, that words cannot even describe it. This is a moment that even God has been looking forward to since creation. It'll be the biggest party that you could ever imagine, and that's just for starters.

Jesus promised he would come back to get us. But when people asked him to tell them exactly when, he said he didn't know. He said no one but his Father knew the precise time. So if Jesus didn't know the day or the hour, we can't even guess (though lots of people have tried) what day it will be or what time of day it will be. The good news is that Jesus *will* come back for his people. Just as he said he would.

ZOOM IN

- The Old Testament talks about Jesus coming as a man, dying, and rising from the dead. It also talks about Jesus' return to earth.
- The Old Testament predicts that the first time Jesus came he would be a "suffering servant" who would serve us at great cost to himself.
- Both the Old and New Testaments give us details about the days before Jesus' return, the second coming of Jesus, and about the final judgment of God.
- The second time that Jesus comes, he will arrive with trumpets blaring as a triumphant "Reigning King." (Quite an upgrade from a suffering servant, huh.)
- The prophet Isaiah said that Jesus would be called: "Wonderful Counselor, Mighty God, Everlasting Father and the Prince of Peace." These names so inspired the composer Handel that he composed *The Messiah*, and choirs around the world have sung these words for hundreds of years.
- The New Testament mostly talks about the future when Jesus will return and how we should live until then.
- The predictions about Jesus and the final judgment in the New Testament agree with the ones from the Old Testament.
- We can know for certain that: Jesus is coming back for us, he will reign, final judgment will happen, and all Christians will spend eternity with God.

- Big fancy words to describe two different time periods in the future . . .
- *Rapture:* When Jesus comes to take only Christians off the earth. It could happen any time. It could happen in one of the following ways:
- ***Pretribulation:*** The belief that Jesus will come and get Christians *before* the Tribulation.
- ***Midtribulation:*** Jesus will return for us in the middle of the Tribulation.
- ***Postribulation:*** Jesus will come and get us after the Tribulation.

If it were up to me, I'd choose pretribulation. But that's just me. And we'll just have to see how it ends up happening. The good part is, when the Millennium comes, things will be much better.

<FactoiD>

God is going to make everything new—even heaven and earth. There will be no more death, sin, tears, pain. We will have no reason to be sad. Ever. It will be God's kingdom with God on the throne. Everyone will worship God because that is what we'll want to do as soon as we see him.

- The *Millennium* is a thousand years when Jesus will rule the earth and the Devil will sulk and lick his wounds for awhile (until he meets his ultimate eternal date with a pit of burning sulfur). People differ on which of the three ways the Millennium could occur:

  Premillennial: Jesus will really come and reign for a thousand years and judgment will come afterwards.

  Amillennial: Jesus will not reign literally. He will reign through his church for a thousand years.

  Postmillennial: We are gradually going toward this time of peace on earth. People will eventually become good.

<Factoid>

Heaven is where God is. It's where Christians will spend eternity. And it's not going to be boring. A huge misunderstanding about heaven comes from all the talk about playing harps and sitting on clouds all day. That would put anyone to sleep . . . definitely. No, think of heaven as a huge rock concert with bands and orchestras and choirs with super-sized-symphonic-quadraphonic-surround-sound that is digitally enhanced. The place will be jammin'!

Q: Isn't there any way we can know when Jesus is coming back?

A: We'll never know the exact time, but the Bible does give us some clues. Jesus told about certain things that would occur as signs to warn us when the time was close. Some people like to look for these signs. They keep track of what the Bible says about events happening in the world today and then try to figure out when Jesus will come.

Q: Don't many of the events happening around us today indicate that we live in the last days?

A: They seem to. However, people throughout history have thought Jesus would come back in their lifetime. Even people in the Bible thought that. Lots of events today seem to signal Jesus' return, but no one knows for sure. And we won't know until the day Jesus actually shows up. So get ready, kids; have your bags packed and ready to go at any moment, because it could be today.

Q: Which parts of the Bible tell about the last days?

A: The book of Revelation in the New Testament and parts of the book of Daniel in the Old Testament talk about things to come. The authors of those books, John and Daniel, had visions and dreams about what would happen in the "end times"—very wild and amazing visions that include angels, colored horses, earthquakes, dragons, beasts, thrones, trumpets, lambs, hail, fire, blood, wars, celebrations, weddings, heavenly choirs, and Jesus. They wrote down these dreams and visions to us to give us a glimpse into the future. Most of it is very elaborate and detailed and sometimes confusing. Many adults have a hard time figuring it all out. All we really need to know is that Jesus is *coming back for Christians.*

Q: When Jesus comes back, what will happen to all the Christians who died earlier?

A: All the believers who died will come back to life and, together with all the believers still living, will meet Jesus in the clouds. That's a lot of people hanging around up in the sky.

Q: Will we be spirits?

A: No. We will all have new, perfect bodies. No disabilities, no one will be too short, too tall, too fat, too skinny, or too weird looking. We will still be ourselves and look different from each other, but our bodies will be perfect. Maybe these new bodies will be equipped with wings, or maybe we will be beamed up like Scotty on *Star Trek*, but we're gonna be hangin' with Jesus when he returns.

You wouldn't want to be caught dead in hell. It's an actual place reserved for those who choose not to believe in Jesus. Hell in the Bible is described among other things as blackest darkness, eternal torment, everlasting fire, eternal punishment, and eternal separation from God. No one gets to visit hell and then decide to leave.

The *good* thing about hell is that you don't ever have to go there. If you know Jesus, you won't even have to pass by the gates and hear all the people weeping and wailing and gnashing their teeth, which is what the Bible says they'll be doing. What a creepy place!

BeSiDeS THaT...

- Our bodies are amazing machines. But the body is just a shell. The person you are is not defined by flesh and blood, but by your soul—the essence of what makes you, you.
- After we die, we can count on judgment. It will occur in God's courtroom after Jesus' return.
- There will be no lawyers and no juries. Only a judge—God himself.
- God will look for everyone's name in the Lamb's Book of Life, and for those whose names are not there, this is a day to dread. If you are a Christian your name is in the book. (Do you think we'll be listed alphabetically?)
- This will be the final judgment that will determine who's going to heaven and who's going to hell. After that there will be no moving around. This may seem harsh, but hey, it's not like we were never warned.
- Christians and unbelievers will be judged separately.
- For the believer, this day is nothing to be feared. We will be found not guilty of sin because of what Jesus did for us. God will judge Christians for the good things they've done, and we will get crowns and things—kind of like an awards ceremony.
- For the unbeliever it will be a day to dread, because without Jesus standing between her and God, all God will see is her sin and wickedness. What a horrible moment for those who turned down God's free gift of salvation.
- Finally after everyone has been judged, the Devil will be judged and thrown into a lake of burning sulfur.

What Difference Does It Make?

The difference between looking forward to Jesus' return and not ever thinking about it is:

Having hope and being ready or having no hope and being unprepared.

Remember:

- Jesus could come back any second, so you need to be ready.
- If you belong to Jesus, you can *know* you will spend eternity with him in heaven.
- Heaven will be the ultimate—the most exhilarating, dynamite, awesome, spectacular, and sensational time you've ever had.
- The best part about heaven will be hanging out with God. We'll see what never-ending joy is like.

(*Scripture passages to support this chapter*)

Ask Professor Little

- Signs that will warn us of Jesus' return—Matthew 24:3–29
- We'll have perfect bodies—Philippians 3:21

Factoid

- Hell is described—Matthew 13:42

Chapter eleven

Is Christianity the only true religion?

HiNT

The dictionary defines religion as

belief in a supernatural controlling power

worship of a supernatural power

a particular system of faith and worship

Does Christianity fit this definition? Yes. Do other religions fit this definition? Yes. Are all religions basically the same, including Christianity? No. Religions differ significantly from each other, although they may share several of the same characteristics. Each religion has very specific ideas about what is true.

Other Religions

Is Christianity the only true religion?

According to the Bible it is.

Believe it oR NOt

Christianity is the largest religion in the world.

Christians—about 1.9 billion of them—can be found all over the world, but the majority of them live in North America, South America, Europe, and Australia.

We share the Old Testament with the Jews.

Judaism is the religion of the Jewish people. They study our Old Testament Scriptures. They do not believe Jesus was the Son of God, but simply a good Jewish man. They are still waiting for God to send the Messiah. Though they have their own country, Israel, Jewish people—more than 18 million of them—live all around the world.

Buddhists want to reach nirvana.

Buddhism is practiced primarily in Asia. Buddhists believe that because we want things, suffering is a part of life. They believe the way to end suffering is to stop wanting things. Once you stop wanting things, with the help of the teachings of Buddha, you will reach a thing called nirvana. Once nirvana is reached you simply cease to exist as an individual. There are about 324 million Buddhists in the world.

Muslims don't believe Jesus is God.

People who follow the *Islam* religion are called Muslims. Their holy book is called the *Quran*. They don't believe that Jesus is the Son of God, but that he was merely a prophet. They follow the teachings of a prophet called Muhammad. They believe in the God of the Old Testament but not Jesus. In Islam, heaven is total paradise, which you get to by following certain rules and living a good life. Muslims are found all over the world, but most live in the Middle East and Africa. There are about 1.1 billion Muslims in the world.

Hindus believe you could come back to earth as a different creature after you die.

In the *Hindu* religion there is a never-ending circle of birth, life, death, and rebirth. As soon as any animal, insect, or human being dies, that being is immediately reborn in another form. Whether he moves up or down the scale of life depends on how good he was in his previous lives. If he's been good enough he may go from poor to rich. If he's been bad, he could come back as an ant. This is called the law of karma. Hindus don't eat hamburgers because they think the cow could be a dead relative. Most of the 781 million Hindus in the world live in India.

- God is just a word, unless there is a person behind the name. You need to know how each religion defines God, and what other things its followers believe, before you can say if they are different from Christianity.
- Did you know that the Buddhists don't even have a god? Buddha was a man who lived many years ago. He himself admitted he was not God. He didn't know for sure whether God existed or not. Buddha taught that each person has to find truth for herself and that, even if there were a God, God could not help her. This doesn't sound like the Christian God.
- The Hindus say that everything eventually becomes a part of God. God is not a separate being. We will all become a part of God. The only problem is that you have to live a good enough life to work your way up to becoming a part of God. They believe that you do this over many lifetimes and that you keep coming back until you get it right. This doesn't sound like the Christian God.

- Muslims believe God is personal, like the Christian God, and that he is separate from his creation, like the Christian God, but his name is Allah. Their God is a different God altogether. Theirs is a very distant and not a very loving god. This doesn't sound like the Christian God either.
- The Jewish God is the Christian God. The Old Testament is all about the Jewish people and their relationship with God. They are God's chosen people. The problem is, they do not believe Jesus is God.
- Christianity is the only religion that does not believe you can work your way to heaven (or nirvana). Christians get to heaven through believing in Jesus.

God so loved the world. . . . He cares about us. He loves each one of us.

That he gave his only son. We don't have to find our way to him; he comes to us.

*That whoever believes in him. . . .*This means you, your cousin, your mom and dad, your teacher, the goofball you sit next to, and the nasty person you met last week.

Shall not perish but have eternal life. You are saved. You've been rescued from certain death.

ZOOM OUT

- It doesn't really matter what a person thinks of Buddha or Muhammad because they were just men. They never claimed to be God.
- Of all the great religious leaders in the world only Jesus claimed to be God.
- Jesus is unique because he is God.
- Jesus asked people all the time, "Who do you think I am?" He was trying to get them to say they believed he was God.
- Jesus' followers believe he is God.
- Jesus was a Jew. The disciples were Jews. The first Christians were Jews. But God made it clear that anyone who wished could belong to him, not just the Jews.

<Factoid>

Other religions simply say do the best you can . . . and we'll see. God says you just can't be good enough, so I will offer you this free gift of salvation. All you have to do is accept it. This simple gift that God gives us makes Christianity unique among all the world's major religions.

- Non-Jewish people are called Gentiles. Those who believe in Jesus are called Christians.
- Some Jews believe that Jesus is the Son of God. They are also called Christians or Messianic Jews.
- The Holy Spirit (the Christian God) lives inside his people. No other god does that.
- The Christian God has an incredible love for us. No other god loves us.
- The Christian God gives away salvation for free. No other god does that.

How many gods in other religions do these things?

Send their son to us
Talk to us
Die for us
Care for us
Pray for us
Know us
Create us
Become one of us

Answer: none.

Q: Aren't Christians a little too demanding when they say you have to believe in Jesus?

A: The Bible says Jesus Christ is the only way to God. Without him there is no salvation. Some people complain this is too extreme, that Christians should include other possibilities in their religion. The fact is, Christianity cannot include any other possibilities because Jesus is what makes Christianity. Without Jesus there is no point—no Savior. Think of the Bible without Jesus, God's Son, dying on the cross to bridge the gap between us and God. You would have God, sin, humans, and nothing else. God couldn't reach us and we couldn't reach him. Besides, Christians don't set up the rules of their religion; God does.

Q: Don't other religions have the Golden Rule?

A: The Golden Rule says to treat others the way you want them to treat you. And yes, almost every religion agrees with this rule. It is a good example of a law everyone says he should follow even though no one can do it all the time. However, God offers Christians forgiveness when we fail, and the Holy Spirit helps us become better people. Other religions don't offer these things; other religions leave you on your own.

Q: Does it really matter what you believe? Isn't it more important just to believe in something?

A: It absolutely matters what you believe. Many terrible, horrific acts have been committed by people who believed in what they were doing. Adolf Hitler believed that his race of people was superior—so he killed six million Jews. He was very wrong.

Q: If I believe strongly in something, doesn't that make it true for me?

A: What you are saying is that truth doesn't matter. Consider this question: "How many believe that the sky is green?" It doesn't matter how many people think it is green, the truth is, it is blue. (Okay, if you live in Michigan or British Columbia, chances are it is gray today, but it sure isn't green.) You can't vote on truth. Believing in something doesn't make it true. Not believing in something doesn't make it false. Facts are facts. Before you believe in anything you need to ask, "Is it true?" Truth is truth. Jesus is the Son of God and Buddha is a dead guy. If Jesus is the true God and you believe in Buddha, you are believing in something false.

Q: Why don't Christians let other people believe whatever they want to?

A: People *can* believe whatever they want to. God gives free will, remember? However, because we know how great it is to know a loving God and to learn from our Creator how to live, we want to tell everyone about it. It's like telling your friends about a great movie—you loved it, so you want others to see it too.

BeSiDeS THaT...

- We hear about celebrating diversity. But did you know that God was the very first to celebrate diversity?
- Every person on this planet has value and is unique in the sight of God.
- He pours color into our skin as unique as each individual.
- He gives us faces that look different from each other.
- He gives us personalities that make us individuals.
- God loves every single human in this world.
- He doesn't turn away anyone who comes to him.

Does this celebration of diversity mean that all religious beliefs are to be celebrated? No, it does not. God loves all the people of the world but not all the people of the world love God. Many different religions are in the world, but none of them can fit inside Christianity.

What Difference Does It Make?

The difference between accepting the teachings of Christianity and accepting the teachings of another religion is:

Developing a relationship with the God who cares about you or living a dead-end life.

Remember:

The act of believing in something does not make it true.

People in other religions hope to earn their way into heaven by doing good works. They have to worry about messing up.

Because God loves us, he sent Jesus to earth. Christianity is the only religion that holds up this truth.

Jesus said he is the way, the truth, and the life. The only way to God is through Jesus.

Because of who Jesus is and what he did on the cross, we have salvation. We can spend eternity in heaven.

(Scripture passages to support this chapter)

What Difference Does It Make?

- Jesus is the way, truth, and life—John 14:6

CHapteR twelve

Where do the words *Christian, Christianity,* and *Christmas* come from?

HiNT

Everything about Christianity was, and still is, determined by who Jesus was and what he did. He was: the author of its teachings, the person the teachings are all about, and the center of its salvation message. He is the reason we hope, our power source, the head of the church, and the one who sent the Holy Spirit to believers. It just doesn't make any sense without Jesus Christ. He is the main character, the center of our faith, and its founder. He's the guy that makes it happen. Otherwise you may as well go to Disneyland or to the zoo and hang out with the monkeys on Sundays.

CHRISTIANITY

Where do the words *Christian, Christianity,* and *Christmas* come from?

Yep, you guessed it: *Christ* (which is one of Jesus' names).

Believe it OR NOt

The Bible was not written on a computer.

When Jesus lived on earth—before the Internet, television, telephones, radios, telegraphs, newspapers, and pencils—people did not have as many ways to write out messages as we do. They mostly talked to one another and retold what they heard. They wrote down important information, but it wasn't as convenient as it is today. Writing took lots of time and work. So more people *heard* about Jesus than read about him.

Thousands of people found out about Jesus without ever once checking the Internet for information.

The disciples, who knew him best, split up after Jesus ascended to heaven and they went in all different directions. Everywhere they went they told people about Jesus. And the people they told, told more people. Pretty soon thousands knew about Jesus.

You are reading this book because Christians aren't Beanie Babies.

The first Christians started local churches. It is because of them, and the Holy Spirit, that we have churches today. And because some of them carefully copied the early manuscripts, we have our Bibles. If the whole Christian thing had been a fad that faded away like Beanie Babies or Giga Pets, you would probably never have heard about Jesus, the Bible would never have been written, and you would not be sitting here reading this book. How about that!

Church isn't church.

Christ's church is not a place, it is his people. Jesus said if two or three Christians meet together in his name, he is right there with them. I guess you could call that the smallest church in the world. The biggest church is made up of all the Christians in the world, about two billion people. Christ's church is people, pure and simple.

No building can hold the whole church.

No structure known to man could hold all the Christians at once, even if you could find a convenient time and place for everyone. God's church knows no boundaries. It is totally global. So it's not buildings or denominations. It is the people.

<Factoid>

Names for groups . . .

Kangaroos—a mob
Penguins—a flock
Fish—a school
Cows—a herd
Christians—a church

- Even though Adam and Eve weren't called Christians, God chose them to be his people.
- God picked Abraham to be the father of a great nation, the Jews.
- God promised the Jewish nation that they were his chosen people.
- God extended that promise to all people through Jesus, and now we are his people if we choose to be. His people are his church and his church is his people.
- The book of Acts describes the beginnings of the first church. It started when the Holy Spirit rushed in with tongues of fire. After an event like that, Jesus' followers weren't about to mosey on home to see what was for dinner. No, they stuck around to see what Peter, who had stood up to talk, had to say. After all, he had spent so much time with Jesus. When Peter finished speaking, three thousand people became Christians and were baptized. God's church was born, rock solid, and was revving up for action!
- Most of Jesus' early followers were Jewish, although there were also Gentiles (non-Jews) who became Christians. The followers of Jesus were starting to multiply like crazy!
- One of the new Christians was a man named Paul who used to hate Christians something fierce. But then he had a little encounter with God as he walked along a road out in the middle of nowhere. A blazing light and God's voice booming down on him convinced him to become a Christian right there on the spot. He went on to write practically the whole New Testament. I guess you could say he not only turned over a new leaf, he became a different tree altogether.

- After his conversion, some people were not too pleased with Paul's new agenda. They said he was a troublemaker, he was starting riots, and he was the ringleader of the Christians.
- Believers were first called Christians at Antioch not so long after Paul started preaching.

<Factoid>

In *A Grief Observed*, C. S. Lewis wrote, "It is easy to say you believe a rope to be strong and sound as long as you are merely using it to cord a box. But suppose you had to hang by that rope over a precipice [cliff]. Wouldn't you then first discover how much you really trusted it?" Don't be afraid to put Christianity to that rope test. You need to know ahead of time what you're going to grab for when you find yourself hanging over a cliff.

✦ So what did these Christians do when they got together? They had potluck dinners. It says so right in the Bible. It doesn't say who brought what or what was for dessert, but it says that they ate meals together.

✦ The new Christians practically lived together. They helped each other out and shared everything with each other.

✦ They prayed constantly. Going to potlucks didn't stop them from praying, either.

<Factoid>

Churchy things like steeples, crosses, pews, buildings, baptismals, organs, pulpits, hymnals, and choir lofts are things *people* decided were churchy things. *God* did not invent these things or tell us to invent them. They are okay, but not necessary for his church to be a church.

- They also remembered Jesus by eating bread and drinking wine whenever they got together. Today we call this Communion.
- The disciples who had been with Jesus taught everyone the things Jesus had taught them. Can you imagine hearing people who had lived with Jesus tell their stories? These were not the kind of sermons that put you to sleep.
- Christians in the early church were expected to . . .

  Believe in Jesus Christ

  Be baptized both by water and the Holy Spirit

  Obey the Word of God

  Tell others about Jesus and let them see how he changed them

  Serve others

Just because you can't touch God does not mean that he does not exist.

God will not stop existing because someone says he doesn't exist.

Q: When did Jesus first start talking about the church?

A: Shortly before Jesus went to heaven, he asked Peter, "Who do you think I am?" Peter answered that Jesus was the Son of God. So Jesus said, "Upon *this* rock I will build my church." As far as anyone knows, they were not standing on a huge rock with a steeple and pews built with materials from Home Depot. No, Jesus was talking about Peter's recognition that he was God's son. Everyone in the church needed to recognize this before the church could grow.

Q: Who decided that church services would be on Sundays?

A: The first Christians decided to meet on Sunday, the day after the Jewish Sabbath (Saturday), because it was the first day of the week. It was the day when Mary and Martha found out Jesus had risen from the dead—the first Easter Sunday (without chocolate bunnies, eggs, and baskets; that part's just for fun).

Q: Does that mean Peter was the head of the church?

A: No. The head always was and always will be Jesus. And all the church members are the body parts. Now some may get to be legs, and others toenails, but all the parts are necessary. If someone you know gets to be an arm and you have to be a liver, you don't need to be jealous. Everyone serves a specially-chosen-by-God function in the body of God's church. Because we are all part of one body, if one member is hurt and in pain, the whole body is hurt and in pain. That's why we help each other out and do what's good for the whole body, not just for ourselves.

Q: Why does the Bible call the church the bride of Christ?

A: Before you start thinking that being Christ's bride sounds totally weird (especially you guys), remember that this idea is simply a picture of the church's relationship to Jesus. Those words tell us how much Jesus loves his church.

Q: Is it okay to secretly wonder whether you believe all this Christianity stuff or not?

A: Sure it is. You don't even have to wonder in secret. If you believed everything that you were told and didn't ask questions then you could never really trust what you know. It's important for you to know why you believe in God. You shouldn't believe just because your parents want you to. Believe because it makes sense to you.

Q: What if I can't figure it out?

A: Don't worry. Keeping asking God to show you the truth, talk to other Christians, and read the Bible. Trust me, no one has ever come up with a question that has stumped God or that has brought Christianity crashing to the ground. God will eventually show you everything you need to know. Some things will have to remain a mystery though. The Bible says that there are some things about God we will never understand.

Getting to the Right Floor, an Exercise in Faith

Is faith believing something that you know isn't true? No, faith is believing something that you have decided *is* true. When you step in an elevator and let the door shut and press the little button with the number two on it, you expect that the door will once again open and you will be on a different floor. This is faith. You believe that the elevator will get you upstairs without crashing to the basement because of all the times that you've been in elevators and didn't crash. You have faith that you will be on floor number two because you pressed the number two button. (Now if you wanted to be on the *third* floor and accidentally pressed number two, it is not an issue of faith but rather of number recognition; and if you keep making this mistake then perhaps you should consider using the stairs next time.)

***Ekklesia* . . . That's Greek to you and me.**

The word *church* comes from the Greek word *ekklesia*, meaning "a gathering of people." Christians gather together and form churches in their cities and towns and neighborhoods. All these churches put together are God's church.

BeSiDeS THaT...

- Is it stupid to believe the teachings of Christianity? What if Christians are all wrong? Think it through with the part of your brain that looks at things sensibly. (You do have that brain part, no matter what your big brother says.)
- It is a historical fact that a man named Jesus Christ walked the face of this earth. Jesus said that he was the Son of God—and his life and character showed him to be trustworthy. Christianity starts with the truth that God was his Father. If this is true then the rest is believable.
- Jesus appeared to his followers after his death. He lives on. If Jesus were dead, then none of this Christianity stuff would matter. It would be just something to read about in history books.
- Millions of people have had personal encounters with Jesus throughout history.
- Everybody has needs only God can fill. If these needs could be filled by human inventions then we would surely have figured out by now how to do it. We were created and designed by God.
- Christians become new people when they follow Jesus. Knowing facts about God is one thing, but seeing people become more like Jesus with your own eyes proves the facts.
- God gives us a purpose. We are eternal beings. Eternity doesn't start later, it's already begun. What the world has to offer is temporary; what God offers, we can take with us into eternity.
- Christians know their sins are forgiven. They no longer have to live with guilty consciences, just repentant hearts.
- God gives Christians each other. He has commanded Christians to love each other, help each other, comfort each other, and to hang out together and have fun.

What Difference Does It Make?

The difference between calling yourself a Christian just because that is what you are used to or believing Christian teachings because *you've* thought it through is:

Being embarrassed or having doubts about your religion or fully enjoying the benefits of being a Christian.

Remember:

- Never believe in Jesus just because someone—even if it's your parents or your best friend—says you are supposed to.
- When you conclude from the evidence that *you* believe in Christ, you can start to know him personally. You'll have a terrific friendship with him.
- As you get to know Jesus, you will begin to feel his love for you and you will love him back.
- Jesus will show you how good God is and he'll teach you the truth about things.

(Scripture passages to support this chapter)

Believe It or Not

- Jesus is in the midst of two or three Christians meeting together—Matthew 18:20
- God's church knows no boundaries—Ephesians 1:22–23
- When one member of the body hurts, we all hurt—1 Corinthians 12

Rewind

Chapter 10

- Predictions God makes in the Bible come true 100% of the time.
- The Bible promises that someday Jesus will return to earth and take all Christians to heaven with him.
- No one except God the Father knows exactly when that will happen, not even Jesus.

Chapter 11

- Christianity is the only religion that says you can do nothing to earn your way to heaven.
- Of all the great religious leaders in the world, only Jesus claimed to be God.
- The only way to God and heaven is through Jesus.

Chapter 12

- Christ's church is not a building; it is made up of God's people.
- Jesus is the head of his church and the entire reason for Christianity. Without him everything would be meaningless.
- God chose each of us to belong to him and be part of the church.

What Difference Does It Make?

Spiritual Building Block: Faith

You can learn how to grow in your faith in the following ways:

Think About It: Taking the steps toward finding out for yourself what you really believe is a sign of growing up. This is a fantastic time for you, even if a little scary. When you read *What Difference Does It Make?*, you will find yourself face-to-face with many tough issues that cannot be ignored. As you read the book, take notes: write down questions or ideas that you would like to find out more about later.

Talk About It: See if you can find a group of people (or a partner) to study this book with so that you can all learn from each other. Encourage everyone to be totally honest and respectful of each other as you study Christianity. Remember, everyone is on a journey of faith; we're just at different points on the road.

Try It: If you or others in the group start to believe in Jesus, be sure to have a time of celebration—the angels in heaven will be celebrating along with you. But don't stop there. Encourage each other to move beyond a decision to follow Jesus and to live out the joy of being a Christian.